Dreamtime Magic

Dragonhawk Publishing Titles

General

Treasures of the Unicorn
More Simplified Magic
The Animal-Wise Tarot
Animal-Wise

Beginnings: A Dragonhawk Series

Music Therapy for Non-Musicians
Psychic Protection

Young Person's School of Magic and Mystery

Magic of Believing
Psychic Power
Dreamtime Magic

FORTHCOMING:

StarMagic
Spirits, Ghosts, and Guardians
Faerie Charms
Healing Arts
Divination and Scrying
Word Magic
Ancient Powers

Young Person's School of Magic and Mystery

VOLUME III:

Dreamtime Magic

by

Pagyn Alexander

DRAGONHAWK PUBLISHING   JACKSON, TENNESSEE

A DRAGONHAWK PUBLISHING BOOK

Dreamtime Magic

(Volume III of *Young Person's School of Magic and Mystery*)
Text copyright ©2001 by Pagyn Alexander
Cover copyright ©2001 by Ted Andrews

First Edition

Indexing by Galen Schroeder

ISBN 1-888767-38-3

Library of Congress Catalog Card Number: 00-100044

This book was designed and produced by

Dragonhawk Publishing
Jackson, Tennessee
USA

Dedication

This book is dedicated to my sisters,
Donna and Gretchen,
and in loving memory of our parents.

Table of Contents

Table of Contents (CONT.)

Magical Practices
(Exercises)

Magical Practices (cont.)
(Exercises)

Preface

A Word to Parents and Students

The world truly is a place of great magic, mystery, and wonder. No group of people is more aware of this than our children. They know the rustling of leaves is a kind of whisper and wishing upon a star has great power. They know there really are ghosts and spirits and that their dreams are glimpses into other worlds and possibilities.

Young people have a great interest in the mystical, the psychic, and the magical, but much of what they know has come to them distorted by movies and television or complicated through confusing books that often are written in clouded, adult "New Age-speak." Too often the psychic and magical world becomes a place of fear and doubts rather than a place of wonder and enchantment. Without meeting their unique learning needs and skill levels, or without the right guidance and encouragement, the magic in the child disappears.

From preschoolers to teenagers and college students, interest in the psychic, the spiritual, and the magical is exploding. Parents are more aware than ever that their children are seeing auras, speaking of past lives, and experiencing spirit. Many of our young people are demonstrating healing touch or having prophetic dreams. And yet little has ever been created to encourage this interest or to help develop these skills within the young. What is most often missing is a way of helping them understand and work with their magical abilities and intuitive energies.

Although there has always been a great deal of material available for general development of psychic abilities, most of the materials and techniques are not designed to meet the unique needs of young people. Generally what has been written is for adults, and while some of it may be applicable to young people, a great deal of the material is not suitable for them (and sometimes not even for the adults themselves). Determining what is suitable can be difficult for those who are experienced. For the young and inexperienced, it is nearly impossible.

The creation of the YOUNG PERSON'S SCHOOL OF MAGIC AND MYSTERY resolves this problem. Great care has been taken to develop a unique course of study which can be beneficial and enjoyable for the young person wishing to unfold his or her own inner magic. It will also benefit the inexperienced and young-at-heart adult explorer as well.

To make this even more possible, we have gathered a faculty of delightful and skilled teachers to develop this course of study to guide the young seeker into new realms of possibilities. All are extremely knowledgeable and experienced in teaching both the young and adults. They are experts in their areas of study, and they can demonstrate all they teach. They live the magical life.

As we began to look more closely at all of them, we found they have other unique qualities in common. All of our teachers are well rounded in their education and experience. They are all practical and grounded, and they have a contagious enthusiasm about their work and their life. And most importantly, they have both a sense of responsibility and a sense of humor about themselves, about the world, and especially about the magical life.

Our teachers provide techniques which are safe and productive. Their methods, exercises, and games are intended to develop, entertain, and affirm the magic that exists in us all. Each course in the school supports and adds to what comes before or follows. Through this study, young people who feel "different" will become more accepting of their unique gifts. Their inner gifts will blossom throughout life and the creative contributions of these young people to the adult world in the new millenium will go well beyond what we can imagine!

We have chosen an initial ten subjects, although others will be added in time. We believe these provide a strong foundation for the student and will lay the groundwork for future, in-depth magical development. However, we will not be learning about casting spells or turning enemies into toads. This school is about helping young people find their inner magic and developing it over a lifetime.

If you provide the right teachers with the right methods, the magic will unfold. While many of us as children had to ignore, fear, or hide our special experiences, today's young people can now embrace and understand these happenings. Their experiences can become invitations to a life of great magic and wonder.

For parents, the YOUNG PERSON'S SCHOOL OF MAGIC AND MYSTERY provides a wonderful opportunity to explore spiritual mysteries with their children. This series provides guidance for working effectively with young people exploring what adults were often never encouraged as children to explore themselves. For young people, this series will keep their dreams, their wonders, and their awareness of the possibilities of life forever strong.

We strongly encourage parents to share the experiences and explorations in the exercises with the young people in their lives. Together, we can all nurture and guide each other into new realms of wonder.

Dragonhawk Publishing

Young Person's School of Magic and Mystery

A Complete Course of Study in Ten Volumes

The Magic of Believing
Psychic Power
Dreamtime Magic
Spirits, Ghosts, and Guardians
Faerie Charms
Star Magic
Healing Arts
Divination and Scrying
Word Magic
Ancient Powers

Lesson 1

Lifting the Veil

This morning, right as I was waking up, I saw the faint outline of a giant fish net being pulled tight against the morning sky. In each section of the fish net, there was a star. Some stars were brighter than others, but all of the stars were lined up in rows one by one.

I close my eyes and try to block out this image because it unnerves me. Ordinary stars don't look like this. I count to five and open my eyes. This time, I see the stars have actually lined themselves up in a geometric pattern that looks like a giant runway stretching far out into the great beyond. I can't see a control tower, so I don't know why I think there's an airport close by.

I lay there for a long time trying to remember what I had been dreaming about. Couldn't remember a thing. Nothing from the night before, but I do have a strange feeling that I must have been some place very far away from here.

Dream Journal
February 25, 1985
6:15 a.m.

People have always been fascinated with dreams. The earliest evidence of dream interpretation comes from the Mesopotamians who lived from 3000 to 4000 B.C. This ancient civilization believed that dreams were messages from the gods. They used clay tablets to inscribe dream interpretations so they could preserve their meanings.

Today, many people are still fascinated with dreams. The Aborigines, Australia's native hunters and gatherers, still believe the dream world is an actual place, a spiritual dimension they call *Dreamtime*. To the Aborigines, this second world is as real as the waking world and is taken just as seriously. They use their dreams to connect with their ancestors and consider these dream beings to be more powerful than living people. Sometimes they work with their dreams to change events or to improve the health of the person they are dreaming about. In waking time, they honor their dreams in their songs, dances, paintings, and sculptures.

In this book, you will learn about the dream world and its mysterious picture language. You'll learn about ancient dream rituals as well some modern techniques for dream exploration. Some of these techniques will help you to develop your creative imagination—the source of your inner magic.

You will also learn how to control your dreams so that you change them for the better. As you work with the knowledge gained from your dreams, you will come to understand that the real purpose of your dreams is to help you grow and evolve into your magical self.

What Are Dreams?

When I say the word *dreams*, most of you will think about the pictures or visions that you have when you are asleep. But dreams can occur when you're awake, which is what daydreams are all about. You can also put your mind into a dream-like state when you meditate or during guided imagery or creative visualization. And dreams can also be the things that you wish for or what you hope your life will be like as you grow older.

In this book, when I say we will be working with dreams, I'm talking about our real AND our imagined dreams. Night dreams and daydreams. I make no distinction. One is not more important than the other. It is just that most people, when they hear the word dreams, think of those we have at night. So we'll begin by looking at night dreams since these are the ones that seem most familiar.

The eminent psychologist and dream theorist, Carl Jung, described our night dreams this way:

> A dream is the theater where the dreamer is at once scene, actor, prompter, stage manager, author, audience, and critic.[1]

---

[1]C.G. Jung, tr. R.F.C. Hull, *Dreams* (Princeton, NJ: Princeton University Press, 1974), p. 52.

Dreamtime Science

DREAMING PERIODS DURING SLEEP

Until about the middle of the 20th century, we really didn't have a scientific ex-planation for what happens when we sleep.

Researchers in the mid-1950s learned that when people first went to sleep, the brain waves appeared to be resting (not thinking) for about the first 90 minutes. Then the brain seemed to wake up and start to think while the subjects continued to sleep.

As they slept, after about 90 minutes the eyes of the sleeping volunteers started to move rapidly from side to side under their closed eyelids. Their heart rates increased and their breathing became more rapid. When the volulnteers were awakened a that time and asked what was happening, they reported they were in the middle of dreams.

This discovery had a dramatic impact on the scientific community. Rapid eye movement (REM) became known as the sleep associated with dreams. The other period of sleep became known as non-rapid eye movement (NREM) and was first regarded as non-dreaming time. Most remembered dreams occur during REM sleep, which occurs about every 90 minutes,

Continued research on NREM sleep showed scientists their subjects were also dreaming during these periods, but a different type of dream, NREM dreams are more thought-like. As the scientists transcribed these dreams, it seemed as though the volunteers were telling themselves stories or quietly musing, much as they might do when awake and daydreaming.

Scientific studies also show that animals dream and in all mammals studied, there is evidence of REM sleep.

ERGO:

WHOEVER SLEEPS
ALSO DREAMS!

19

Characteristics of Night Dreams

If you think about it, many of our night dreams have a certain dramatic quality to them, as if you're at a movie or watching a television show. But our night time dreams share other common characteristics, so let's look at them as well.

DREAMS SEEM REAL

Some dreams start in a vaguely familiar place, like your home, school, or at a park. But other dreams can occur in strange places where the scenery changes quickly and things appear to be *very* different from your real life.

DREAMS PORTRAY ACTION

Usually the action in the dream is happening to you, the dreamer. In 80 percent of all dreams, the action involves the lower part of the body. You're walking, running, riding a bicycle, or driving a car. Some dreams can have more quiet action, especially if you haven't been very active during the day. You might even be observing the dream actions and events from a distance.

CHARACTERS APPEAR AT RANDOM

Sometimes you know the characters in your dreams, but other times you don't. Dream characters can change into other people, animals, or things without your doing anything. Some people report dreams where they've seen dead loved ones very much alive. On the other hand, nightmares have terrifying and hideous creatures who are often so ugly that most dreamers have trouble believing these characters are creations of their own mind.

DREAMS REVEAL INNERMOST FEELINGS

Most dreams have some type of "feeling" to them. This can range from mild to vivid, from sorrowful to joyful, from loving to hateful, from confusion to inner peace. Most people don't remember their happy dreams. Instead, people tend to remember dreams where they had intense feelings such as the fear during a nightmare.

DREAMS HAVE THEIR OWN MORAL CODE

Sometimes you do things in your dreams that you would never do in real life, like kissing someone of the same sex, or even a frog. Dream research shows that people who worry about breaking the law sometimes have dreams where they are robbing banks or killing people. Some psychologists believe these types of dreams help us to fulfill disguised but unacceptable wishes which we can allow to be active only during sleep.

Different Types of Dreams

Dream researchers believe that about 80 percent of our dreams are trying to provide useful information about the problems we are facing in waking life. However, the time of night has a lot to do with the kinds of dreams we have and whether they deserve our attention.

CLEAR-THE-AIR DREAMS

These kinds of dreams usually have little significance and are not important enough that you need to work with them.

Daydreams

There are two types of daydreams. Although all daydreams have some benefits, not all need to be focused on and worked with. You can deliberately make up things you wish in order for something to be more special in your life. This kind of wish daydream is common, but is not usually important enough to work with. Or a daydream can just happen and these are the ones you'll want to pay attention to. The second type is usually more meaningful because they can show your innermost hopes, yearnings, and wishes of the heart.

Physical Dreams

Physical dreams are usually caused by something physical and can occur at any time during the night. This type of dream alerts you to something that is happening in the physical world. You may dream of a doorbell ringing and wake up to find someone at your door, ringing the bell. Or you might dream that someone is trying to suffocate you and wake up to find yourself with one of your blankets on top of your head.

In both situations, the dream images were caused by physical things that needed you to take note. Since the causes of both of these dreams were something physical, they can usually be forgotten as soon as you answer the door or shove the blankets off your face. Physical dreams are usually not the kind you need to work on.

Housekeeping Dreams

When most of us go to bed, our minds are still racing from stress, worry, or anxiety. In order to help us relax, our first dream of the night involves a sorting through the mental and emotional clutter of the day. That's why some of the early dreams in the night seem to be an "instant replay" of our previous day's activities. This sorting of memories helps the mind and body relax by releasing those useless concerns of the day.

Sit-Up-And-Take-Notice Dreams

These are the kinds of dreams that often require you to look closely at the imagery to figure out the message.

Analytical Dreams

In these dreams, we see ourselves for who we are in our waking life. Usually we are looking at how we are interacting with what is going on around us. This type of dream provides us with useful information on how we are living our lives.

The action in analytical dreams occurs as a story instead of a mere rerun of the previous day's activities. We seem to be sorting through the memories of the day's activities and then analyzing how this day has gone compared to other days.

Analytical dreams usually come in a series and seem to give us several different ways of looking at the same

What Researchers Have Learned About Dreams

☆ Everybody dreams every night, but many people have a hard time remembering their dreams when they wake up.

☆ Age, gender, sex-role orientation, and social class affect dream content. Elderly people, for example, have fewer characters in their dreams.

☆ Stress, traumatic experiences, emotional difficulties, drugs and medications, or illness can cause nightmares.

MALES

Men's dreams seem to take place more often outdoors and are often more aggressive than women's. Men's dreams involve more male characters than female. Men also report more sexual activity and more rejection in their dreams.

FEMALES

Women's dreams take place more often indoors or in settings with enclosed places. They often have an equal number of males and females. Women often dream about people they know and involve friendly interactions with the women, often helping or protecting other dream characters.

CHILDREN

☆ Children five years old to adult spend approximately 20 percent of their time sleeping. As people get older, the percentage of time dreaming drops off to as low as 13 percent in some people.

☆ When asked, many children may report they have never had a happy dream. The more sensitive the child, the more prone he or she is to nightmares.

thing. While they don't actually provide solutions to our problems, they can give us great insight into who we are and how we are responding to situations around us.

You will definitely want to work with your analytical dreams when and if you remember them. Even if you only remember a smidgen or two of an analytical dream, hang onto it because it is usually a clue to how you can solve your problems more effectively in waking life.

Nightmares

Most people know what a nightmare is, but they may be unaware that there are two kinds. Dream research shows that for most older teenagers and adults, the nightmares that occur before midnight usually have a physical cause. If, before midnight, you dream of a monster stabbing you in the stomach with a knife, you may have a simple case of indigestion.

After midnight, nightmares tend to stem from emotional tension. Once our bodies have relaxed, we're ready to look at the root cause of our problems in waking life. These after-midnight nightmares are meant to "thump us on the head" and get us to wake up and see how some situation in our everyday life is making us miserable. Rather than telling you there is something wrong with you, nightmares usually try to show what is wrong with a situation in your life that you are ignoring or hiding from.

𝔇ream 𝔯iðiculus

Daffy Dream Definitions

Automobile

To dream that you ride in an automobile denotes that you will be restless under pleasant conditions, and will make a change in your affairs. There is grave danger of impolitic conduct intimated through a dream of this nature.

If one breaks down with you, the enjoyment of a pleasure will not extend to the heights you contemplate.

To find yourself escaping the path of one signifies that you will do well to avoid some rival as much as you can honestly allow.

For a young woman to look for one, she will be disappointed in her aims to entice someone into her favor.

Outdated definitions from a book by
Gustavas Hindman Miller,
Ten Thousand Dreams Interpreted, 1909

People tend to remember their nightmares so they are a wonderful place to begin dream work. Your job in understanding your nightmares is to become aware of what lessons you might be missing and learn how to do something about them. For those of you who are bothered by nightmares, you'll learn more about them in Lesson 7, "Fighting the Monsters Under the Bed."

Recurring Dreams

People who have had bad experiences such as surviving plane crashes or natural disasters like floods or tornados often have recurring dreams. People who have been in a war or exposed to extreme violence may relive the experiences in dreams for months or even years.

When the same dream happens on a fairly frequent basis, it is called a *recurring dream*. Like nightmares, a recurring dream usually appears after midnight and happen for the same reason nightmares do—we haven't taken action on some problem in our waking lives, possibly sometime in the past. Recurring dreams tend to show up from time to time until we eventually work through the situation.

Guidance or Teaching Dreams

According to Betty Bethards, author of *The Dream Book*, we usually have one important teaching dream each night. In these dreams we are given specific information about a problem we are facing in our daily life.

If we find ourselves talking with a teacher, an advisor, or a counselor, we may be experiencing a teaching dream. In some teaching dreams, we are actually sitting in a classroom hearing a lecture or attending some type of school. At other times, we might be standing near a platform or at a podium almost as if we are presenting a report or giving a lecture.

Besides finding ourselves in a classroom type of situation, teaching dreams often give us information we've never heard before or which seems new when we dream about it.

Extraordinary Dreams

Extraordinary dreams are those with content so re-markable we "just know" on some level these dreams serve a special purpose. These more magical dreams connect us to other dimensions where we do things that are beyond our everyday experience. We talk with animals, heal a friend, or view future happenings. We might even chat with loved ones who are no longer living.

How Is Magic Connected to Dreams?

At night, while you are sleeping, your dreams hold up a magical mirror that only you, the dreamer, can see. When you look into this mirror, you can see an honest reflection of yourself, the real you—not someone you'd like to be.

By looking into this magical mirror, you can learn more about yourself and the world around you through your dreams. At first, this very honest look at yourself can be a little confusing and you might even dislike what your dreams are saying about the way you are living your life. But as you get to know yourself better, you'll also discover that deep inside of you is a truly wonderful person.

By following the techniques described in this book, you will learn how to use your dreams to tap into other levels of awareness that are far greater than our everyday understanding. In this way, dreams can serve as a direct link to the Divine or the essence known as God, the Great Creator, or Universal Spirit. This access provides links to wisdom, knowledge, and guidance you couldn't get otherwise.

As you work with your dreams and put their messages into action, you can cause your energy to shift. You become a bit more confident. You become a bit more perceptive and more able to understand the world around you a little better. It is as if the veils are lifting.

That is when the magic simply begins to happen.

By reading this book, you've already shown that you are curious about your dreams. If you are at all nervous about starting to work with your dreams, I strongly encourage you to look at Lesson 8, "Precautions and Protections." There are a few safety procedures you should be aware of in that lesson and these will ease your mind if you're new to dream work.

Now, let's begin to lift the veils!

Imagine if...

- your magic was sparked by curiosity and work with your dreams,

- your dreams rewarded you with positive experiences,

- your dreams showed you where you needed help,

- you accepted your dream messages, both the good and the not so good,

- you understood the magic in your dream images,

- you could use your psychic power to control your dreams,

- your creative imagination grew with every daydream and nightdream, and

- every dream experience was a special gift to you.

Awaken the magic in your dreams!

31

*Magical
Practice*

Creating a Dream Journal

**skills
developed**
- strengthens dream recall
- provides a persoanl history of dreams
- enhances creativity
- increases communication with the spirit world

In order for magic to happen in your dreams, it's absolutely critical that you begin to record them. It is only by recording your dreams over a period of time that you can get them outside of yourself so you can look at them more objectively at a later date. By keeping a dream journal, you also send a powerful message to your Higher Self (the inner magical and spiritual part of you) that you are committed to learning more about what it has to say about your daily life.

Your dream journal provides a space where you can tell the story of how your dreaming-self evolved. Over the years, your Dream Journal will become an historical record of your personal life symbols, giving you access to the very special person you are growing up to be. Your dreaming life is very different from your waking life, but your dreaming life provides you with a unique perspective on your waking life.

In the exercise that follows, you will record a recent dream in your Dream Journal. If you do not already have a dream journal, here are some things to consider in keeping one. Your Dream Journal is a very private tool, so look over the suggestions here and use what's comfortable for you.

☆ **Your Dream Journal can be handwritten, typed, or tape recorded.**

I like to write my dreams in longhand, but that's me. Many people find it helpful to type their dreams. Other people use a tape recorder.

There was a time when I tape recorded my dreams during the night. It was a totally different experience from writing about dreams. The first time I heard my voice, it was a weird experience and I didn't necessarily like the fact that I sounded a little dorky, as if I were talking from a distant star. But as I listened to the tape recordings of my dreams, I realized I could "actually hear" what was going on rather than just writing about my dreams. I loved how that worked because I could easily tell the emphasis my dreaming mind was trying to capture. This gave me a unique perspective on the dream images and my thoughts at the time.

I stopped tape recording my dreams because I found it too difficult to wake up in the middle of the night and start talking. That act of talking tended to wake me up and then I had trouble getting back to sleep. This might not be a problem for you.

33

Magical Practice

☆ **You might want to have two notebooks.**

I find it helpful to use two notebooks. I keep a spiral-bound notebook on the night stand near my bed. If I wake up and want to write about a dream, I have figured out a way to reach over in the dark and scribble down the main details without turning a light on. Later in the morning, I use another spiral bound notebook, which is actually my dream journal, to write about the dream, filling in the details.

As I write my dreams, I divide each page in two parts and use the left-hand column to record the dream and leave the right-hand column blank. When I'm ready to interpret the dream, I make notes in the right-hand column about the meaning of the dream. This method works for me, but you might find that some other method works better for you.

☆ **Use the sample dreams at the beginning of the lessons as guidelines for writing about your dreams.**

In this book, I've provided examples of my dreams in each lesson. This will give you an idea of the level of detail I try to capture when writing about my dreams. In general, I just try to write about what happened in the dream. If I can't remember what happened next, I make three dots (…) on the page to indicate lapses in time or places I couldn't recall the details. Sometimes just the act of making those three dots is enough to bring the dream back into my memory.

Write or tape record the date, and if you know it, the time the dream happened.

Creating a Dream Journal (cont.)

THE MAGICAL PEN

- *find a quiet place where you won't be disturbed*

1. **Write about any dream that you can remember.**

   This could be a scary nightmare from your past, a
   dream from your childhood, or a more recent dream.

2. **Write about the dream in whatever way it comes to
   you.**

   Don't worry about sentence structure or grammar.
   Just try to record the dream, getting down as much
   written information as you can.

   It is a good idea to record your dream in present tense,
   as if you were experiencing the dream now as you
   write about it.

As you write about your dreams, do NOT
try to turn them into stories with a
logical beginning and a linear sequence. Just describe what happens in
your dreams and you'll do just fine.

35

Magical Practice

3. **Be sure to describe any feelings or emotions you experienced during the dream.**

   If you have trouble remembering your feelings during a dream, ask yourself:

   How did I feel when (some action event) was happening?
   Did my feelings change in the dream?
   How did I feel when I woke up?

   EXAMPLE:

   *As I was running through the forest, I **felt like** a wild stallion fleeing for his life. When I saw a clearing in the woods, I **knew** which way to go.*

4. **Write about any thoughts you had during the dream.**

   If you said something to yourself during the dream, try to record what you said.

   EXAMPLE:

   *As I was fighting the dragon, I **said to myself,** "Hey, I'm pretty good with this sword! Wonder where I learned to do that?"*

Creating a Dream Journal (cont.)

5. **Write about any other things you want to remember about this particular dream.**

    ☆ thoughts or "knowings" about this dream,

    ☆ questions about this dream that still bother you, or

    ☆ ideas you have about what this dream might mean.

    EXAMPLE: :

    When I woke up, I knew Grandma was o.k. now. She was no longer in pain and that there really was a place called Heaven.

If you'd like, take time to write about other dreams you've had. Do skip a page or two though because we will be doing some additional work on this dream in Lesson 4.

SUGGESTIONS FOR PARENTS

Be Curious About Dreams

➤ **Keep an open mind.**

If your child or teen has come to you with this book and is asking for your help, try to keep an open mind. As a parent, you are now being called to offer some real guidance and spiritual direction.

This may come at a time in your own life when you feel most uncertain and afraid, especially about your own dreams. Try not to worry. What your children often need most at this time is for you to simply listen and to encourage dream work.

➤ **Work with your child.**

Even if you and your teen are already talking about really personal things, dreams are personal and sharing them can make most of us feel vulnerable or exposed.

➤ **Respect your child's emotions.**

Keep in mind that very young children (up to three or four years old) usually cannot distinguish between dreams and waking life. Between four and six, children can begin to tell the difference, but may still have difficulty in understanding that dreams come from inside of them.

Between five and eight, children are usually able to understand that dreams happen inside themselves and they are better equipped to work with their dreams.

➤ **Start your own Dream Journal.**

Many kids are exposed to journal writing at school and will like the idea of the two of you starting a Dream Journal. If you live in colder climates, some families have found that winter is a good time to begin a project like this because during the winter months dreams are generally more vivid and easier to recall.

Whenever you start, make it a special occasion so that your son or daughter will feel more comfortable about working with you on his or her dreams.

➤ **Be mindful of your role in dream work.**

As a parent, your child looks to you for support and guidance. Don't try to be your child's teacher on this topic. The magical exercises in this book provide a framework for learning.

Many of these exercises were intentionally created to challenge your child's critical thinking abilities. Because of this, your child might start asking you some very tough questions and may even challenge some of your very basic beliefs. If and when this happens, try to remember that this is a good thing. It is a sign that your child is ready and willing to grow up.

Lesson 2

Getting Started with Dream Work

In my dream last night, I saw Dad. We were at the house that he was building when he died. "See that tree over there, Peggy," Dad says while pointing to an old mulberry tree near the edge of the woods. "I always wanted to build you a tree house in that tree. I feel bad about not getting around to doing that. Guess I just ran out of time somehow."

We walk over to the tree and stand beneath it. He encourages me to climb it and I do. I feel the wind in my hair as I climb up to the set of branches that was, at one time, my favorite place to "perch." Leaning back against the tree trunk, I look down to see if my father is still standing there. He is. He still looks the same as he did when I was eight years old. Dark skinned, broad shoulders, and glasses. He smiles and waves at me. I smile and wave back. I feel so at peace. I close my eyes and fall into a deeper sleep.

As I start to wake up, I hear my father's voice say to me, "Honey, don't ever forget that you can do whatever you set your mind to do."

Dream Journal
June 12, 1976

My father died when I was eight. Like so many kids whose parents die when they are young, I struggled for a long time to make sense of why this had to happen. The night he died, my father came to visit me in my dreams. He told me he was O.K. and that he was no longer in pain—his old war injury was gone. He just wanted me to know that he loved me very much.

Dad's funeral was very confusing. I couldn't understand why, if my father was alive last night in my dreams, he didn't get up and climb out of that casket. But then Uncle Red explained things to me by saying, "Peggy, sometimes they visit us in our dreams. This doesn't mean that they are alive; it simply means that they exist in another dimension." Uncle Red went on to tell me that Dad had visited him the night before as well. After that, Uncle Red just sat there with me holding my hand while I cried and cried. I don't know for sure, but I think Uncle Red was crying too.

The whole idea of my father visiting other people the night he died really freaked out my mother. For one thing, he didn't visit her. They were divorced at the time, so I could understand why he stayed away.

My sisters couldn't remember if Dad visited them that night. They both hoped he hadn't forgotten them, but they just could not remember any of their dreams from the night before. Dad's sister said he didn't visit her, but she sure hoped he'd drop by sometime.

Over the years, I've come to realize that I was raised in a very special way. My father's mother, Grandma Lu, was a clairvoyant. This means she had the gift of second sight. My mother was always a little nervous around Grandma Lu and Grandma Lu never did very much to help mom feel more comfortable. Since my mother never really got along with Grandma Lu, it was not un usual for me or my sisters to go along with my father to her house without my mom.

Of course, my sisters and I loved it when Grandma Lu would have one of her "visions." At my grandparent's house, it was pretty normal for me to hear about a deceased relative who had dropped by for a visit during the night. Guess that sort of explains how psychic phenomenon and seeing deceased loved ones in dreams seems pretty normal to me.

In this lesson we will explore some of the mysteries and wonders of dreams. And hopefully, we will begin to answer some more of your questions about this amazing world of dreamtime.

The Most Powerful Magic of All

In the *Magic of Believing*, we learned the most powerful magic of all was the power of our thoughts and our beliefs. We also learned:

> What we think, do, and believe on one level always affects us on other levels—physically, emotionally, mentally, and spiritually. This means that all parts of our lives are connected and that there is a cause and an effect relationship to everything. Magic simply reveals those connections.[1]

Our thoughts and beliefs affect how we feel about ourselves and how others feel about us. Even if we merely react to something in our lives, we create a

---

[1]Ted Andrews, *Magic of Believing*, (Jackson, TN: Dragonhawk Publishing), p. 22.

Imagine if...

- what we believe affects our dreams,

- we really are like what we see in our dreams,

- our dreams reflect what is going on while we are awake,

- our dreams about other people are not just about them,

- great possibilities are revealed to us in our dreams, and

- our dreams are a magic mirror.

Dream great possibilities!

thought, feeling, or belief. During the course of our lives, what we have created in our thoughts and beliefs develop into a life force of their own and start to influence how we live our lives. This includes influencing our dreams:

> For thousands of years, people believed that it was physically impossible for a human being to run a mile in four minutes. But on May 6, 1954, Roger Bannister broke the four-minute-mile barrier. Within the next year, 37 more runners followed in his footsteps, and 300 more the year after that. Now runners do it all the time.[2]

Roger Bannister succeeded because he simply didn't buy into the assumed limitations of the human body. As he ran, did he just simply forget everything except his belief in himself and his ability to break the world's record? Most likely. When Roger broke through the four-minute-mile barrier, he created a new belief about the human body. Others soon followed in his footsteps.

Roger Bannister lived a magical life because he made his dreams come true. If we can dream it, then we can do it or be it. Like my father said to me in my dream: "Honey, don't ever forget that you can do whatever you set your mind to do."

Our dreams hold up a magical mirror so we can look into and see ourselves as we really are, not as who we want to be. This same magical dream mirror can also

---

[2]Excerpted from *Psychology for Kids,* by Jonni Kincher, © 1995. Used with permission from Free Spirit Publishing, Inc., Minneapolis, MN. All rights reserved. Phone: 1/800/735-7323. Web site: www.freespirit.com.

show us how our thoughts or beliefs affect our waking lives, how our dreams "mimic" our waking lives, and how other characters can sometimes mirror or reflect different aspects of ourselves.

Thought or Belief?

I don't know about you, but sometimes, the craziest things can slow me down. I mean, I think I know what I'm talking about, but then someone will ask me about the meaning of a word and whoosh! I'm back to the dictionary, looking up what Noah Webster had to say about things. So what IS the difference between a thought and a belief? In my *Webster's New Elementary Dictionary* (New York, Amer-ican Book Company, 1965), it states:

> **thought** n 1: the act or process of thinking; 2: serious consideration (give thought to the future); 3: power of reasoning and judging; 4: power of imagining or comprehending; 5: a product (as an idea or fancy) of thinking (idle thoughts) 6: the intellectual product or the organized views and principles of a period, place, group, or individual.

> **belief** n 1: confidence that a person or thing exits or is true or trustworthy: FAITH, TRUST (belief in Santa Claus) (belief in democracy) 2: religious faith: CREED 3: something that is believed: OPINION

Dictionaries are a wonderful place to begin. By looking at these two different definitions side by side, we can quickly see that thoughts are connected to an intellectual process (thinking). Beliefs, on the other hand, are about what we think or know to be true with absolute certainty without having to think about it (such as the "givens" or things assumed in a debate).

By their definitions alone, you can probably see that our beliefs are more powerful than thoughts. Once a belief gets inside us, it sticks like glue. Our beliefs tend to color our thoughts and we will intentionally block out things that don't match what we believe. The harder we believe, the more narrow we become in our thinking. So let's look at how we get our beliefs and what that means in the scheme of things—especially in our dreams.

FAMILY BELIEFS

Did you ever notice how many people—our parents especially—will occasionally say some things in a way that it sounds like everybody believes as they do? For example, when I was a kid, I heard my parents say the following things about money: money is the root of all evil, a penny saved is a penny earned, good people pay their bills on time, successful people make lots of money, and money can't buy you happiness.

You may have heard similar comments in your house. All of us have inherited some basic beliefs about money. If you look at what I heard about money, they hardly

Dream Ridiculus

Daffy Dream Definitions

Masks

To dream that you are wearing a mask denotes temporary trouble, as your conduct towards some dear one will be misinterpreted, and your endeavors to aid that one will be misunderstood, but you will profit by the temporary estrangements.

To see others masking denotes that you will combat falsehood and envy.

To see a mask in your dreams denotes some person will be unfaithful to you, and your affairs will suffer also.

For a young woman to dream that she wears a mask foretells she will endeavor to impose upon some friendly person.

If she unmasks, or sees others doing so, she will fail to gain the admiration sought for. She should demean herself modestly after this dream.

Outdated definitions from a book by
Gustavas Hindman Miller,
Ten Thousand Dreams Interpreted, 1909

make any sense. Some even contradict one another. No wonder I grew up a little confused about money. Can you tell me how "being good" relates to paying bills on time? Do you think they were saying that if I saved money, I would grow up to be unhappy or even evil?

Please don't misunderstand me. In no way am I saying that we shouldn't listen to our parents. When we are young, we need our parents to guide us and tell what we need to do so we can stay out of trouble. Things like, "Don't touch that stove or you'll get burned!" Now that statement was very helpful. But sometimes the advice we got as children, the things that we were told, just don't seem to fit as we get older.

And what about those other people besides our parents who also had a chance to influence our thoughts and our beliefs? Have you ever read a book that changed the way you looked at the world around you? What about your teachers or your boss? What about a television show or a movie? Your friends? If you're in your teens, your friends may have more influence over your thoughts and beliefs than your parents.

At some point, all these thoughts and beliefs coming at you from so many different kinds of people can get very confusing. Sometimes it's hard to figure out exactly what you believe and what you don't. Besides, there's all this pressure to grow up and to stop acting like little kids.

FAMILY DYNAMICS

In Lesson 1, you learned that people dream differently based upon their gender and their age. But you don't need to read lots of research information to understand that people dream differently. Think about your own family. Do you have at least one family member who's very different from the rest of you? Maybe you are like me. In my family, I was the one who was a little "different" from my two sisters.

First off, I was the youngest. My sisters were only a year apart and had many of the same interests and the same set of friends. They shared a room and made me swear that I wouldn't go in it unless they were around. When we were kids, we'd sometimes run around the house and yell or scream loudly at each other to see who was strongest and who could get her way. I was famous for my temper tantrums, for slamming doors, and for arguing at the dinner table.

Most people have at least two ways they differ from other members of their family. They differ by the order in which they were born and they differ by the role they play within their family. The order of your birth within your family gives you a certain family position. Are you an only child, the first born, a middle child, or the baby?

Because our family tends to shape many of our beliefs, our birth order and family role can sometimes box us into a way of being or behaving that might not always be comfortable for us. Generally, older children are expected to care for the younger children whether they like that role or not. Sometimes a middle child is expected to break up the fights between older and younger children. You might want to examine how your birth order affects your relationship with other members in your family because this can all show up in your dreams.

Sometimes the tasks and duties you've been assigned within your family don't feel very comfortable. And sometimes when this happens, we assume a front that may not be who we really are on the inside.

GROWING-UP WISHES

Sometimes, as parents, we forget that our kids can be smarter than we think. When you were younger, you probably had some very fine beliefs. You probably had lots of ideas about the world—how you'd change it and make it a better place to live. If you're like me, you probably even talked with your parents about what you wanted to be when you grew up.

When I was five, someone read me a children's book called *Nurse Nancy*. I instantly fell in love with this character and wanted to do what she did when I grew up. But I wanted to be a doctor instead of a nurse. When I played with my baby dolls, I'd make them all be sick. I'd hold them and sing to them and they were cured somehow.

My mother grew worried about this type of make-believe and so one day she said to me, "Peggy, you can't be a doctor. Little girls grow up to be nurses, not doctors. But maybe you can marry a doctor someday."

As long as you can
envision the fact that
you can do
something,
you can do it—as
long as you really
believe it
100 percent.

Arnold Schwarzenegger,
three times Mr. Universe, actor,
and an Advisor to the President's Council on Fitness

"But MOM! I don't want to marry a doctor. I wanna BE a doctor!" And with those words, I quickly stomped out of the room.

Our parents and teachers see us differently. Their ideas about our futures can be radically different from the one we envision for ourselves. Sometimes our parents base their ideas upon our strengths. But sometimes they base their thoughts about what we should do when we grow up upon what their parents told them.

Back in the 1950s, there weren't as many women practicing medicine as there are today. So when my mother said I could grow up and be a nurse, she may have been trying to help me focus on my interest in medicine and the job opportunities for women in those days. Or she might have simply been repeating what she heard her parents say about some of her career choices.

When it comes to your wishes and dreams, try to think more like you did when you were five or six. You may have known yourself a little bit better back then. Those wishes and beliefs often still show up in your dreams today!

All People Wear Masks

All of us have at least two sides: a public, outside self, and a private, inside self. Everyone at times will take on a *persona* or image of ourselves that may not be who we really are on the inside. Persona comes from the Latin word *per sonara* which means "to speak through." Some people refer to a persona as a mask because at one time, masks were used by actors on the stage and they "spoke through" them as they played their various parts.[3]

The mask or persona we use depends upon where we are, what we are doing, and who we are with. Some personas are made up from our role within our family, such as peacemaker or caregiver. But sometimes we assume a persona from one of our more negative qualities and we wind up acting as the bully, the wimp, the know-it-all, or the troublemaker.

For the most part, personas are helpful because they give us a safe and predictable way of dealing with various situations in our lives. Maybe your friends are pressuring you to do things you don't want to do. In these situations you might assume a persona to literally hide those inner qualities you don't feel comfortable letting others see.

Sometimes we hide behind this persona because we are afraid other people wouldn't like us if they knew who we really were inside. For example, as a kid, one of my personas was "the good student." I never wanted my teachers, fellow students, or friends to know that at home I was known as "the temperamental one" although I'm sure this aspect of me sometimes showed through at school.

At school, my sisters and I were known as "good students." But, at home my middle sister was also the "overly-sensitive one" and she'd cry at the drop of a hat.

---

[3]Kincher, p. 30.

54

She still does and now that my older sister and I have grown up just a little, we try not to tease her too often.

Now, my oldest sister always wanted to be a teacher. From the time I was old enough to sit in a chair, she would play school with me. By the time I was four, she had taught me the alphabet, how to write my name, and how to read little stories.

But my oldest sister was a strict teacher. There was none of this business about bringing my sick little baby doll to class with me. So some days I just stayed home to tend to my babies. But unlike real teachers, my oldest sister didn't care when I did that. She and my other sister would just laugh at me and then they'd go off to play what big girls play when they don't have to watch "the little brat." It was all part of our personnas. But oh, what fun we had!

You Dream Without Masks

Behind the various kinds of masks you present to the outside world through your physical body, there is another inside self watching what is going on. During the day, all kinds of things can happen, and you may or may not notice them. Your outside self or physical self can be busy doing one thing, but out of the corner of your mind's eye, your inside self can be taking in a great deal more. The inside self rarely misses anything going on around you and will often— through your dreams— reveal those things you might have missed as you went through your day.

During the waking day, many of us tend to handle things on a purely physical level, especially when things go wrong. Depending upon your personality and family situation, some things you did during the day to get what you wanted may have been successful and some may not have. Working through your chosen persona or mask, some of you might have slammed doors or thrown things to get your way. Sometimes using your emotions is easier and you may have cried, yelled, or pouted until you got what you wanted. Maybe you even tried logic or fast talking to wear other people down. Many times these actions don't solve the problems and when you start to fall asleep, all of the things that happened during the day will come out of the corners of your mind and you'll begin to dream about them.

When you first fall asleep, both your outside self and your inside self lie down to rest. But about 90 minutes later, your inside self wakes up and you'll start to dream while your physical, outside self remains asleep. Your inside self reviews all the things you've seen during the day, reviewing what went right and what went wrong.

The you in your dreams wears no masks and has no personas. Basically, this inside you doesn't have the usual social armor (your masks and personas) to protect you from the truth about yourself. As your dream unfolds, the clothes you wear, the things you do, and the feelings you have are meant to give you some very big clues as to what is happening in your waking life.

In Lesson 1 you learned that at night while you are sleeping your dreams hold up a magical mirror—a mirror only you can see. When you see yourself in your dreams, this is the *real* you—where all your thoughts and beliefs come tumbling out of hiding and may actually surprise you, where you may not be the person you think you are or the person your parents want you to be. The magical practice that follow will help you learn more about this real self within and what you truly believe about yourself.

As you learn more about the real you and your beliefs, it will be easier to understand your dreams and to uncover the magic within!

*Magical
Practice*

Mirror, Mirror on the Wall

**skills
developed**
- promotes self-knowledge
- increases introspection and reflection
- provides a reference point for dream work

In this magical exercise, you will be using your dream journal and taking a closer look at the differences between your inside self and your outside self. The idea here is NOT to psychoanalyze yourself, but come to recognize the different roles you play in your family because they will show up in your dreams.

You'll begin this exercise by looking at the order of your birth in your family. Think about your feelings about this. We know you had no choice in the matter, but now that you're here, what does it mean to you?

You'll also be looking at your role within your family, your assigned tasks and duties. You may not have any control over this role, but you will be thinking about your feelings about his role. How does it relate to the roles of other members of your family?

Finally, you'll start to explore your different personas. You might have a persona made up of some of your very real qualities, such as the creative kid or the extra sensitive one. Depending on the situation, you might find you wear a mask to hide some qualities you don't want others to see. A persona can be positive—a loving son or daughter, an artist, a good student. It can also be less than positive—the bully or the wimp.

Sometimes it is easier to hide behind our masks because we are afraid people won't like who we really are. Other times, we are pressured from our family or friends to wear a mask even when it is uncomfortable for us. Because the role of peacemaker or caretaker so often found in families is a very difficult one, the people put into these roles can sometimes grow weary of always having to put other people's needs before their own. Our dreams can show us what personas we are comfortable with and which ones aren't working for us and need to be changed.

In my family there were just three girls. My oldest sister and I were both pretty flaky little kids, the kind who were so busy paying attention to other things that we'd bump into walls or get lost in a crowd. That type of stuff really scared our mother. So one day, my mother put my middle sister in charge of the two of us. Well, my oldest sister really didn't like that, so she would find every opportunity to dig at our middle sister. Before long my oldest sister had said something nasty that hurt our middle sister assigned the caretaking role and she'd be crying. Our middle sister really was very sensistive and was always crying about one thing or the other anyway.

Magical Practice

This probably sounds like things were pretty awful at my house and I'll admit things did get a little tough at times, but all in all, my sisters and I were very, very close. Even though we fought like crazy, we loved each other even more. And now that we've all had time to grow up and get out on our own, we've all learned how to love each other differently, this time as friends.

Careful...

Don't confuse wearing a mask or having a different persona with multiple personalities, a rare disorder best determined by a psychiatrist. Wearing a social mask is a generally healthy way to deal with various situations in your life.

If you realize you are wearing a mask that is wildly different from the real you, talk to an adult you can trust. There is probably a reason for the mask you may have not understood. Talking things over can help you understand why you use the mask and even help you see if the mask is no longer needed and you are ready to let it go or give it up.

Mirror, Mirror on the Wall (cont.)

If you do this exercise and realize that some of the different family members aren't getting along, try not to worry too much about it. Sometimes family members don't get along because they have different interests or there is too much of an age difference. Sometimes family members don't get along because they're too much alike. And sometimes family members don't get along and even after they are grown and gone, they still don't share much besides being from the same family. These things can't be helped, but just as with my family, as awful as it may sound as we describe what we did, we have learned to be friends.

Does that mean that my caretaker sister gave up her role? No. Did my oldest sister and I stop being flaky? Maybe a little. Did my oldest sister quit picking on my caretaker sister? No way! Do they both still boss me around like I'm some little kid? For sure!

If you discover that you really are wearing a mask that you don't like, that's pretty normal. If that happens, then it is a signs that you might need to make some changes in your life. We'll talk more about making changes and solving problems in the magical practice in Lesson 5, "Doing Homework in Your Sleep."

Magical Practice

**BEHIND
THE MIRROR**

1. **On a blank page in your Dream
    Journal, put the date and make
    notes about your family situation:**

BIRTH ORDER

I am (an only child, the youngest, a twin).

> Describe how your family treats you because
> of this position.

FAMILY ROLE

In my family, I am (the caretaker, the peacemaker).

> Describe what's expected of you because of this
> role in the family.

Mirror, Mirror on the Wall (cont.)

2. **Make notes about who you are at school or work.**

    MY PERSONAS

    At school, I am known as (the class clown, a nerd).

    > Describe what kind of mask you might wear because of this school identity.

    > Describe what this mask allows you to hide about yourself and why you might want to hide this part of yourself.

    At work, I am known as (a hard worker, an honest worker, a reliable worker).

    > Describe what kind of mask you might wear at work because of this identity.

    > Describe what this mask allows you to hide about yourself and why you might want to hide this part of yourself.

3. **Make notes about who you are when you are with your close friends, the people you trust.**

4. **Describe how you want people to see the "real" you.**

5. **Add any additional information you think might be important.**

Magical Practice

6. Leave four or five blank pages in your Dream Journal so you can add additional thoughts about your personas at a later date.

7. Write down the last dream you remember.

8. When you are finished recording the dream, consider the following questions and write about them in your Dream Journal.

   Don't worry if you can't describe these roles exactly, but do write your feelings about the dream even if you can't really see the roles clearly.

   Did you act differently than you would have in your waking life?

   From your perspective, what was your role in the dream?

   Did the other people in the dream seem to treat you as if you were in a particular role?

   How did these other people treat you compared to how you think they would normally treat you in your waking life?

You are led through
your lifetime
by the inner learning
creature,
the playful spiritual
being that is
your real self.

Richard Bach
Illusions: The Adventures of a Reluctant Messiah

SUGGESTIONS FOR PARENTS

Accentuate the Positive

➤ **Tell your children what they are good at.**

Children can never hear enough about what they do well. If they have a natural talent, let them know it. You don't need to brag or praise them lavishly. Just describe what you like, avoiding judgmental words. For example you might say "you are really great at telling jokes— I sure wish I had your talent!"

➤ **Talk with your kids about your birth order.**

Talk with your children about your birth order and how that has affected your life. If you are an only child, share what that feels like. Did you ever wish for brothers or sisters? If you had brothers or sisters, talk about how you all got along. Did you argue with them?

Be honest, but try not to dwell on issues that you haven't been able to resolve on a persona level. If possible, keep things a little on the light side.

➤ **Talk about your role in your family as you were growing up.**

Children love to know what their parents were like at their age. Do you still have to play a childhood role

when you visit with your family? Share only those things
that are age appropriate and keep it light. Use your
childhood stories to teach by example and give your
children as much insight as possible into how you are
alike and how you are different.

➤ **Talk about the many roles or personas you sometimes
need to use.**

As an adult, you are sometimes required to play a role
that isn't always comfortable. Perhaps you feel a need to
be the good parent or the caring boss. In addition, you
may be the emotionally strong one for some of your
friends. If possible, share this information with your
kids and how you feel about wearing all these different
roles.

Be mindful of how much you disclose to very young
children. They many not have the wisdom to understand the somewhat strange dynamics of a business
world or some of the popular jargon like dysfunctional
family.

➤ **Schedule time for dream sharing.**

If you're not doing so already, schedule some quiet time
with your kids where all you will talk about is dreams.
Some parents find that breakfast is a good time for a
quick sharing of dreams, but other parents find that
breakfast is just way too hectic for this type of activity.

It's O.K. if you only get together once or twice a week
for dream sharing. Some people find it easier to do
this activity on a weekend when there might be more
opportunities for spending time together.

Lesson 3

Learning
Dream-Speak

Well, I could hardly call it a dream. I'm standing in a room filled with total darkness. Someone comes in and turns on the lights. I can't see who this someone is, but I feel a male presence standing behind me and a little to my right. This presence hands me a black and white photograph. It's a picture of a woman alone in a woods standing near an old oak tree. As I look at the photograph, it comes to life and the woman bows to the tree and I know that she is performing some type of sacred act. That's when I hear the voice behind me says, "Follow her lead!" Then suddenly, the light goes out and I am once again surrounded by total darkness.

Dream Journal
August 12, 1993

Our dreams can seem very real. On some intuitive level, we know our dreams are about us and what is happening in our lives. If we're lucky enough to remember even a part of our dreams (and often it's the scary dream parts we remember), we can try and figure out what this dream may be trying to tell us that is so very important

Each night our dreams speak to us about our lives. Understanding dream-speak, the way your dreams communicate with you, is the key to understanding what the dream is saying. Dream messages are sent from yourself to yourself in unique ways.

Imagine if...

- your dreams really do speak to you,

- the places your dreams take you mean something,

- your angels and spirit guides talk to you, and

- the colors in your dreams mean something.

Become fluent in the language of your dreams!

In waking life, you probably send messages to your-self all the time, either silently or out loud. I usually call this as "talking to myself." Sometimes I don't even know I'm doing it. There I am just going about my business and suddenly my mouth opens up and I'm carrying on this audible conversation with myself. Usually, I'm tell-ing myself things to do or asking questions. If I can't find my car keys, I'm likely to say out loud:

> Okay, Pagyn. Just slow down and think about things. Where were you the last time that you had your car keys? What were your doing?

Usually these questions are enough for me to figure out where my keys are.

The Language of Dreams

Our waking language uses words to convey our thoughts and is very evolved. When we speak to one another, we no longer need to draw pictures in the dirt or speak with our hands to signal what we mean. In-stead, we communicate through sentences, paragraphs, questions, and answers. Language helps us to talk to one another about things without having to draw pictures.

There are times, though, when what we are trying to convey in words goes beyond what we can communicate in normal everyday conversation. This is especially true when we try to use words to express our feelings and our emotions. Sometimes our actions tell more about what we're feeling than our words. Sometimes we can't find enough words to say all that we mean. Sometimes we can find no words at all to express our feelings. Sometimes words just get in the way while the spaces between have more meaning than the words themselves.

DREAM IMAGES AS METAPHOR

In waking language, when we can't find the words to express our feelings, we turn to music, poetry, or art. These forms of expression seem to somehow fill our need to communicate our feelings. The pictorial, figurative language used to write poetry is similar to the language used in our dreams. Both rely on *metaphor* to convey meaning, a figure of speech in which a word denoting one object is used in place of another to suggest a likeness between them.

> A wave of appreciation washed over me when
> I realized he remembered my birthday.

In this sentence, the word *wave* saves you the trouble of having to describe the attributes of a wave to make your point about how your appreciation felt.

Dream-speak is primarily metaphor. Images are used to act out a message through a scene or an activity. It might help to think of dream language like a game of charades. In this game, ideas are acted out by a team of people playing while the other team tries to guess the word or phrase. If you've ever played charades, you probably know just how dramatic some people can get when acting out the name of a movie, book, or play!

Our dreams are a bit like the game of charades, but if we don't know much about dreams, we may not even know there's a message for us. Many people are unaware that each dream image is carefully constructed so we can relate to it personally. Even if we know there may be a message there for us, the action sometimes moves so quickly we miss the point. If only our dreams would tell us something like:

☆ this picture of you driving your car represents (is a metaphor for) your journey through life

☆ this picture of your sitting in a boat crying represents (is a metaphor for) your lost love

Dreams are not a photographic reproduction of what is happening in your waking life. They are much more. Your dreams are YOU expressing yourself in a very personal and poetic language. And this is why the magical dream mirror is so important.

When you look at your dream images, you need to remember that the characters, actions, exaggerated emotions, and dream symbols are mirroring, or reflecting, information back to you. Depending upon what is happening in your dream, a person, place, or thing may not be what it first appears to be. These images may be symbols reflecting something else—even some part of you—just as metaphors do. A person causing you problems in your dream may represent something causing you problems in your waking life, although the dream image is not an exact replica of the real situation.

Don't turn away from
possible futures before
you're certain that you
don't have anything to learn
from them. You are always
free to change your mind
and choose a different future,
or a different past.

Richard Bach,
Illusions: The Adverntures of a Reluctant Messiah

DREAM IMAGES AS SYMBOLS

In your waking world, you see and use picture images or symbols constantly, but you probably don't think much about them. Symbols are a bridge between thinking and doing, serving as a short-cut method for conveying information. For example, when you see a red hexagon sign with the word STOP written on it, you immediately know what to do:

> STOP. Look in both directions. If nothing is coming in either direction, then continue.

Sure, when you were very young, someone had to tell you what the stop sign meant, but after that, whenever you saw one, the meaning was very clear. That's the beauty of symbols. You don't have to think too much about them, they quickly convey a lot of information without a lot of words or lengthy explanations, and they can mean the same thing to a large group of people.

Most of the time in our waking life, we can relate to a symbol or a picture representation more quickly than we can relate to written or spoken language. Let's pretend for a moment that you've been transported to an airport in another country and the people there do not speak your language. Could you look at the symbols below and figure out what you needed to do so that you could make a telephone call?

Sure, you could!

Because there has been great care given on an international level to make certain symbols easy to understand, people can travel to other countries with relative ease. We can also get more done because we're not wasting time asking for directions or trying to learn a foreign language just to make a simple phone call or mail a letter. In our waking life, seeing a familiar picture or symbol is comforting to us. Many times we count on various symbols or pictures to guide us safely through our day.

Picture symbols work the same way in your dreams as the well-known symbols around you, but they can also have a special meaning that is unique to you and to you only. In dream work, all symbols can be placed into one of three basic categories:

☆ conventional,

☆ personal, and

☆ universal.

The table on the opposite page provides more detailed information about these three basic kinds of dream symbols.

Three Types of Dream Symbols

Conventional

Images and symbols that have the same accepted meaning to everyone. Everyone seeing them thinks of the same thing, such as the American flag and a STOP sign. You already know and understand what these symbols stand for so you don't need to think about their meaning when they appear in your waking life or in your dreams.

Personal

We relate to things differently depending upon our personality, our likes and dislikes, and our experiences with people, places, or things. This is unique for each of us whether we are awake or dreaming.

If you were studying for your driver's exam when you had a dream with a stop sign in it, then the dream would have one meaning. But if you dreamt of a stop sign on the day that you just got a ticket for running one, then the meaning would be different. The symbol and its conventional meaning hasn't changed but what's was happening in your life has and colored the meaning of the symbol for you at that time.

Universal Symbols

These images are widespread throughout many cultures and shared by all people all of the time. All over the world, eggs are seen as a symbol for birth. If you see an egg in your dream, you can easily recognize your dream probably has something to do with new birth or a life change that is about to unfold. The butterfly is often seen as a symbol of transformation or change.

Eggs, butterflies, and other universal symbols will mean the same thing to people all over the world regardless of their nationality or religious tradition.

Beginning Work with Dream Symbols

If you haven't ever worked with symbolic imagery before except perhaps in literature classes, the idea of one thing representing something else can be a little hard to understand. But if you take the time to think and study your dreams, then you can usually begin to see what they are trying to say to you.

Your dreams can come from all aspects of your life. Sometimes, you'll dream about the previous day's activities. Some dreams will show you a childhood memory or you'll see people from your past. Other dreams will use images from television shows, movies, or even religious symbols to catch your attention.

In attempts to communicate, your dreaming self will use any person, place, or thing you are familiar with or have an attitude about to get the message through to you. Of course, you need to remember there is a very good chance that none of these people, places, or things are what they appear to be. After all, this is a game of dream charades, and we all play our part.

When we use the magic dream mirror to understand what our dreams are saying to us, look at three things in particular: where you are, what you are doing, and who you are talking to. These details and what they represent are the keys to understanding the dream's message.

WHERE AM I?

The dream setting is the physical location in which the dream is taking place and provides the emotional backdrop. It sets the tone, the time, and some physical conditions for how the dream sequence will unfold. The location of a dream offers a definite clue as to what the dream might be about.

> If you dream that you are back in your childhood home, then in all probability you are dreaming about something in your current life that is an echo of your childhood. Many adults continue to have the same nightmare they had when they were little children. This simply means that your subconscious is till experiencing the same fear or issue that was a challenge when you were a child. The "monster" may have a different face now in your waking life, but the psychological dynamic will be roughly the same.[1]

When you look at dream settings, it is best to consider them symbolically, to step back from the details and see the bigger picture and perhaps remember your feelings about the setting. Dreams about being at a shopping mall may have more to do with searching for something that will FIT your needs than it does with buying a new OUTFIT. Or dreams about being back in grade school may have to do more with going backwards in time than writing your ABCs.

When you look at dream settings, always begin by looking at what that location means to you on a per

---

[1]Excerpted from *Dreaming Insights* by Gillian Holloway, ©1994. Used with permission from Dr. Gillian Holloway, founder of Lifetreks, Vancouver, WA. All rights reserved. Web site: www.lifetreks.com.

Dream Ridiculus

Daffy Dream Definitions

Telephone

To dream of a telephone foretells you will meet strangers who will harass and bewilder you in your affairs.

For a woman to dream of talking over one denotes she will have much jealous rivalry, but will overcome all evil influences.

If she cannot hear well in conversing over one, she is threatened with evil gossip, and the loss of a lover.

Telescope

To dream of a telescope portends unfavorable seasons for love and domestic affairs, and business will be changeable and uncertain.

To look at planets and stars through one portends for you journeys which will afford you much pleasure, but later cause you much financial loss.

To see a broken telescope or one not in use signifies that matters will go out of the ordinary with you, and trouble may be expected.

Outdated definitions from a book by
Gustavas Hindman Miller,
Ten Thousand Dreams Interpreted, 1909

sonal level. Perhaps for you, being back in grade school is a return to happier times when you had a teacher who loved little children. Perhaps when you see yourself in this dream, you are more able to remember who you were and what you wanted for your life back then.

Wherever you find yourself in your dreams, the background location helps to pinpoint the specific area of your waking life your dream is trying to emphasize.

WHAT AM I DOING?

Even though words are often used in our written and verbal communication, they only tell a small part of the story. Almost everything we really understand about what others are trying to say comes through our nonverbal communications. Consider this old folk saying.

Actions speak louder than words.

No matter how much we try to hide from it, our bodies never lie. Actions in our dreams tell us a great deal about what is happening in our waking life.

The body has a language of its own—gestures, postures, and actions. Do you fold your arms across your chest if someone picks on you? Has someone ever avoided looking you in the eye when telling you something? Have you ever suspected when something was amiss? Gestures, postures, and actions can have great meaning no matter how small they may be.

Let's say you have a dream in which you seem to be lost. Say you're at school. But as you walk down the hall way, you can't seem to remember why you're there. You can't find your locker. Wasn't the school gym next to the cafeteria? In the dream, you keep wandering around, a little dazed and confused. Your being lost, of wandering around confused, is the key to this dream's meaning.

When you look at the actions in your dreams and compare them to your waking life, it's a little easier to see. If you're wandering around in your dreams a little confused, spend time reflecting upon where you are a bit confused in your waking life.

Being chased is also a common dream. Usually with these dreams there's fear of whatever is doing the chasing. You are probably also feelings helpless, powerless, and want to simply get away from that person, place, or thing. Where in you waking life are you feeling like this?

Many teens as well as grown-ups can have difficulties with authority figures or handling criticism, which can sometimes manifest as dark shadowy figures or monsters in their dreams. So if you dream of being chased or stalked by an ominous force or something is coming at you in a threatening way, look at your waking life and reflect on where you feel you are being threatened or having difficulty with authority figures. In Lesson 7, "Fighting the Monsters Under the Bed," you'll learn how to face your fears and those things that chase you in your dreams.

One of the major goals of magical dream work is to use your dreams to help solve your problems. By considering how dream actions reflect your waking life, you can usually discover some meaning in their messages. You have now started problem solving in your dreams.

Who Am I Talking To?

In many dreams, you'll find yourself talking to other people. Some dream conversations can appear to be meaningless. You're back at school or at work talking about the same old, same old…. The problem with these types of conversations is they are so boring you probably sleep right through them. That's good. Often these unimpressive dreams are meant to relax the body, sort of like watching a movie or television. They shake off the stress and tension accumulated during the day.

With our more memorable dreams, we should take a closer look at what's going on. Often we can find various kinds of patterns by looking at who and what we interact with. As we examine how the characters in our dreams speak to us, look at the following things:

☆ self talk,

☆ heated discussions and arguments,

☆ pep talks and spiritual directions, and

☆ animal encounters or ficitional or mythical beings.

Self Talk

Not too long ago, I dreamt that I was asked to carry several very heavy boxes up a flight of stairs. Although I managed to successfully do this, I remember at one point sitting down on the steps and saying to myself: "Oh! Man! That box nearly broke my back!"

This dream was an exact parallel of what was happening in my waking life. In my job, I was being asked to carry out several very difficult assignments. On the day I had the dream, I had been asked to do something I did not agree with morally. I tried to reason with my boss about what I was asked to do Well, o.k, I may have been a tad bit argumentative, but I had some points I was trying to make. On the way home from work, I started to seriously consider whether or not this was the right job for me. So for me, this dream didn't need much in the way of interpretation. I could easily see the link between what I was feeling in my dream and what I was feeling at work.

Sometimes you'll think or say something to yourself in a dream. In most cases, when we hear ourselves speak in our dreams, we are usually making important comments about our waking realities. With dream self-talk, the meaning is very direct rather than symbolic. Therefore, whenever you recall something that you said in a dream, try to record it in your dream journal. Try if at all possible to make a special effort to look at your comments to your self in your dreams in relationship to your waking life.

Dream Puns

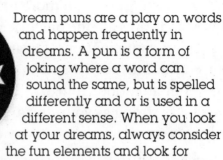

Dream puns are a play on words and happen frequently in dreams. A pun is a form of joking where a word can sound the same, but is spelled differently and or is used in a different sense. When you look at your dreams, always consider the fun elements and look for puns or plays on words. Sometimes these will provide additional clues as to how your dreams relate to your waking life.

For example, how would you write the following if someone in a dream were to say to you:

Is it: *Go get your dress red ...*

Or: *Go get your dress read...*

Would you immediately think that whoever said this had mistakenly meant to say, "Go get your red dress?" Or would you stop and consider the second spelling? Could this dream be telling you something about your waking life and your red dress?

From time to time, when you go back and reread your dream journal, the puns will become more apparent. Please be sure to keep track of your dream puns. I have a separate section in my Dream Journal where I record them. The same pun can show up in other dreams.

Heated Discussions and Dream Arguments

Sometimes you may feel very uncomfortable talking about your dreams because they deal with emotions. With some dreams, you may feel overwhelmed with the feelings, sensing they are more than you can handle. However, dreams are the one place you are free to feel and act out your emotions. Dream emotions are often exaggerated. This adds a sense of drama and is intended to get your attention. Your waking emotions probably won't be as strong as your dream emotions, but most likely they are related in some way to your waking life.

Perhaps you felt very upset with another person about something, but were unable to express your feelings then. Since you didn't consciously acknowledge you were hurt or angry, you repressed or buried your feelings. During your dreams, though, you are free to feel whatever you were trying to avoid during the day. The exaggerated emotions in your dream help you catch the day's feelings, allowing you to play out what was unexpressed in your waking life. So pay close attention to those heated discussions and arguments in your dreams!

Sometimes the action of the dream may appear to be more about someone else than you. Just by looking at the questions raised in the dream "Arguing with Aunt Millie," you can probably already see how Aunt Millie is really a magical mirror reflection of some situation that in your waking life. Aunt Millie really isn't Aunt Millie. She's actually a stand-in for you or someone in your waking life who is acting like a know-it-all.

Arguing with Aunt Millie

Let's say you've just awakened from a dream in which you were arguing with Aunt Millie. Since you haven't seen Aunt Millie in years, this dream doesn't make much sense. Besides, Aunt Millie is no longer living. All you remember about Aunt Millie is that she was something of a know-it-all in real life. You really never liked her much.

So what's this dream all about? First, since Aunt Millie is no longer living, you know this dream probably isn't about what happened yesterday. Since you were arguing, you already know the dream involves strong feelings on your part. You are arguing with an older adult who might have once been something of an authority figure in your life.

Aunt Millie may seem like the main character in this dream, but actually this dream has more to do with you than Aunt Millie. Because you remember Aunt Millie as being something of a know-it-all, we could go so far as to say this dream is trying to show you something about a know-it-all personality in your waking life. With those thoughts in your mind, you can try thinking about the meaning of this dream by asking yourself:

★ Did you challenge Aunt Millie when she was around or did you give in to her?

★ In some area of your waking life are you:
  ☆ acting a little like you acted when Aunt Millie was around,
  ☆ acting a little like Aunt Millie, trying to be something of a know-it-all,
  ☆ is someone else—perhaps an older adult or an older, authority figure—acting like a know-it-all?

★ Do you feel like having a fight or arguing with Aunt Millie or this person she represents?

Dreams are
journeys to
the realm of
wonder!

Pep Talks and Spiritual Direction

I frequently have dreams with a shadowy presence I can't really see, like the character in the dream at the beginning of this lesson. I knew the other presence was real. I've done enough work with my dreams to know this was definitely not some aspect of myself that I didn't want to look at. Can I tell you the name of the other presence or for certain who it was? No. But, I can give you two good guesses. This presence was either one of my spirit guides or my guardian angel.

SPIRIT GUIDES

Spirit guides are similar to guardian angels, but they act more like consultants. They show up in our dreams when we need special advice on a given topic. Sun Bear, A Native American shaman, taught that guardian and protective spirits visit us in dreams. These spirits may tell us about things that are happening in the world around us or they may take us to different parts of the universe to show us new realities.[2]

Usually, spirit guides won't tell you what to do, but instead, give you options. Some spirit guides encourage a kind of question-and-answer approach that allows them to teach you things. Sometimes in dreams you'll meet with a spirit guide in a classroom setting. Or a spirit guide can be just a voice answering your questions.

---

[2]Sun Bear, Wabun Wind, and Shawnodese. *Dreaming with the Wheel.* (New York, NY: Fireside, an imprint of Simon and Schuster, 1994), p. 31.

Understanding what the spirit guide has to say is fairly easy because the conversations are pretty much like your normal, everyday, wide-awake ones. You ask a question and you get an honest answer. Spirit guides are persistent. If you don't like the answer you're given in one dream, most spirit guides will figure out some clever way to help you get the message in another dream.

GUARDIAN ANGELS

My father's mother, Grandma Lu, was a devout Catholic. To Catholics, guardian angels are at the very core of their spiritual beliefs. At my grandparent's house, I couldn't sit in a chair without leaving a little space for my guardian angel. Catholics even have a religious holiday called the Holy Guardian Angel day. To someone of the Catholic faith, a guardian angel is considered a messenger of God. Here's Grandma Lu's explanation of how this worked:

> Talking to your guardian angel in a dream is something like talking with God. If you're troubled about something, your guardian angel can take your message to God. It may take a couple of days for you to get the answer, but don't worry about that. You'll always get an answer somehow, someway. Usually it comes in another dream.

Grandma Lu's beliefs have influenced mine. To this day, I continue to strongly believe in guardian angels and sometimes mine talk to me in my dreams. When you begin to work with your dreams, you too will get guidance from spirit guides, angels, and even more unusual beings.

Animal Encounters, Fictional Characters, and Mythic Beings

It's not unusual for me to have a dream where I'm talking with an animal, a fictional character, or a mythic being. Perhaps this happens to you as well.

Animals tend to fascinate people because they are so closely tied to Mother Nature. Because of this link, animals are symbolic of a greater power and energy. In many fictional stories and myths, animals sometimes speak to humans. Sometimes they are teaching us how to do things; sometimes they do things for us:

> If we dream of an animal, it is the same as having actually encountered it while awake. We need to treat the appearance of an animal in our dreams just as significantly. We should study it. The nice thing about dream animals is that by looking at where the dream scenario took place and who else was in it, we can get an idea as to what part of our life this animal applies.[3]

---

[3] Ted Andrews. *Animal-Wise*, (Jackson, TN: Dragonhawk Publishing, 1999), p. 40. In this book, you can find a marvelous guided meditation called "Dream Totems." This exercise is great for increasing the vibrancy of your dreams. You can also use it to discover the animal that can guide you through the dream world.

The same thing is true for fictional characters or mythical beings who appear in our dreams. If you watch a great deal of television, go to movies frequently, or listen to radio on a regular basis, the fictional characters, mythical beings, and actors or actresses you see there become part of your subconscious.

Seeing yourself in a dream where you are kissing a beautiful actress or a handsome actor can be a fun way to spend an evening. And no, these types of dreams do NOT mean that you want to leave your boyfriend or girlfriend. A dream like this could simply mean the actor is reflecting a person in your waking life with similar qualities. Make a list of the famous person's best qualities. Does anyone in your waking life fit that list?

The famous person, fictional character, or mythical being can also represent an unfulfilled need in your current life. Sometimes, if our lives become too routine or too boring, we need a little spice and romance to bring back those qualities we miss. Is there anything lacking in your life? Are you longing for something?

As with other things in your dreams, take a look at who you are speaking with and what that might relate to in your waking life. People often reflect traits of certain animals. Think of how often we see jokes or cartoons about pet owners who look or act like their pets.

Gillian Holloway offers this piece of information about animal dreams that you might find helpful:

It is common for unpleasant characteristics of loved ones or coworkers to be represented in dreams as frightening or disgusting animals. If you dream that you are sleeping with a rat, for example, take another look at your partner. What have you been afraid to see? Or, if you have no partner, are you "in bed with someone" in the business sense? Check your feelings about the animal, look for dream puns in its name, and look for any possibility of its representing a part of yourself of which you have been afraid or scornful.[4]

In this lesson, you've learned the difference between the language of your dreams and the way we speak when we're awake. You've learned a few new things about the magical dream mirror. You've learned that sometimes different dream images can mirror or reflect different aspects of yourself.

In the magical practice that follows, you will begin to develop your own dream-speak skills and begin laying the groundwork for understanding the messages in your dreams. A whole new world will open for you!

---

[4]Excerpted from *Dreaming Insights* by Gillian Holloway, ©1994. Used with permission from Dr. Gillian Holloway, founder of Lifetreks, Vancouver, WA. All rights reserved. Web site: www.lifetreks.com.

Magical Practice

Follow the Yellow Brick Road

skills developed
- increases overall sensitivity to symbols
- provides a reference opint for dream images

Right now, before you read any further, close your eyes and think about your favorite color. Got it? Now think of all the things that come in your favorite color. Can you see them? How do they make you feel inside?

☆ warm and happy,

☆ soft, like you're ready to curl up for a nice nap,

☆ excited—you're ready for a party!

That's the beauty of colors, especially your favorite one. They help you feel your emotions. What you feel when you see a particular color will depend upon your experiences with it. Even though you may not realize it, many people use color to talk about their feelings in waking life.

I'm feeling a little blue today.

He sees the world through rose-colored glasses.

Her eyes are green with envy.

My! My! Isn't she just all red with rage!

Most people don't think of color as a dream symbol because they are often associated with objects or things in dreams. But if you think about it, color plays a significant part in understanding dreams, especially when the colors change.

By now you should be getting the hang of how these magical practices work. Yes, it's once again time for you to grab your Dream Journal. This time, you'll want to think about your favorite color and what it might mean if you saw it in a dream.

COLORING YOUR
DREAMS

1. On a blank page of your Dream Journal, write the date and the heading "Colors and What they Mean to Me."

   Take some time to write down the following questions and your responsed in your Dream Journal.

2. What is your favorite color and what does it means for you?

   Try to use as many adjectives as you can to describe it.

Magical Practice

3. Write down things that your favorite color comes in.

    Try to include different kinds of objects, vegetables, minerals, man-made objects, things you see on television.

4. If you were to see your favorite color in one of your dreams, what do you think it would mean?

5. What is your least favorite color and what do you think it would mean to you?

    Again, think of things that come in your least favorite color: vegetables, minerals, and man-made objects.

6. Write down the things that your least favorite color comes in.

7. If you were to see your least favorite color in one of your dreams, what do you think it would mean?

Follow the Yellow Brick Road (cont.)

8. Refer to the table on the following pages and compare your feelings about color to those suggested by the experts.

   Depending on the shade of a color, the meaning can vary. In some definitions, you may even find some contradictory meanings.

   Always trust your feelings and your intuition. You, as the dreamer, are the only person who can determine what a color might mean in your dream.

9. Make notes about how you feel about the colors listed in the table included here.

Magical Practice

COLORS AND THEIR

	Red	**Orange**	**Yellow**
IF A FAVORITE COLOR	You are courageous, energetic, passionate, and bold. You may also tend to be a little reckless or impulsive at times.	You may be ambitious, competitive, and outgoing. You might even be an effective leader. Because you have a warm nature, you can inspire others to reach their higher potentials.	You are intellectual and like to use your mind. You may like to invent things or be creative. You can be a little too analytical, but also tend to be spirituality-oriented.
IF IN A DREAM	This "doing" color can indicate strength, health, vigor, courage, energy, or sexual love. May also be related to anger. If a dark red, may indicate aggression or tension. Can indicate danger, and need to slow down and proceed with caution.	This "expansive" color can indicate a need for social acceptance, attraction, encouragement, kindness, or further exploration. May also mean there is a need for more balance and discrimination.	This "happy" color can indicate joy, light, happiness, or intellect. May also be related to cowardice or "yellow-bellied."

Follow the Yellow Brick Road (cont.)

Associated Meanings

Green

You enjoy tradition and authority and are probably a good student and a solid citizen. You may enjoy making things grow, including financial things and things associated with Nature.

Blue

Most likely you are patient and persistent and are good at making rational decisions. You appear to others as poised and dignified.

Purple

You might be sensitive and refined and have high standards. You are trustful of the future and can think in abstract ways.

This "growth" color may be the "green light" needed for you to move ahead. Can indicate new growth, health, healing, and good luck. May also be tied to jealousy, as in "green with envy."

This "spiritual" color can indicate truth or openness. Darker blues may indicate dignity, ambition, or impulsiveness. May also signify a need to go inward. Can be a sign you have gone inward and are feeling "a little blue" or introspective right now.

This "seeing" color can indicate power or the ability to transform or change. Dream may be prophetic, spiritual, or have an intuitive meaning.

SUGGESTIONS FOR PARENTS

Pay Attention to Dream Images

➤ Talk about the earliest dream you can remember.

Even if the first dream you can remember was a terrible nightmare, take the time to share this with your kids. This will help them realize that you are open to hearing them talk about their dreams.

Even though many teens are not always eager to share their thoughts with their parents, there are very few who can resist the temptation to listen intently to someone else's dream. We all do this naturally, secretly hoping that we will learn our dreams aren't so weird after all.

➤ Start talking about your dream images.

Again, it is very important for you to talk about your dream images. Try to approach dream images as if you were trying to learn a foreign language. As you talk about your dreams, try to answer the three W's:

- Where am I?

- What am I doing?

- Who am I talking to?

➤ **Take turns identifying personal and cultural symbols.**

Encourage your children to make a list of the cultural symbols found in their school, classroom, church, or the grocery story. Do this yourself.

When you are with your children in public places, ask them to observe what is going on around them. Then ask them to identify personal and cultural symbols.

➤ **Talk about what colors make you think of.**

Maybe blue makes you think of peace and red makes you feel a little jumpy or excited. There is scientific evidence about how colors affect our feelings. For example, bubblegum pink is believed to calm people down and has been successfully used in dentist offices, in hospitals, and in prisons.

Experimenting with colors can be fun. Place different pieces of colored construction paper on the bathroom mirror for a week. Ask each family member to make notes about how they feel when they see that color. At the end of the week, compare notes and see what the family has learned.

Lesson 4

Interpreting Dreams

In this dream, I driving my car. It's late at night and the fog is so thick I can hardly see. I'm nervous and turn on the radio for a little company, but only get static. Suddenly, the battery on the dashboard starts to flash and then it becomes a solid circle of bright red.

I think about slowing down, but I'm not sure if I have a flashlight or jumper cables in the car. I can't remember when I last saw another car and start to have a deep, sinking feeling in the pit of my tummy.

I pick up my cell phone to call my husband, but as I push the numbers I realize that it, too, is dead. Feeling even sicker to my stomach, I pull over to the side of the road and roll down the window. A blast of fresh air wakes me up.

Dream Journal
"I'm in a Fog"
August 12, 1999

Each night our dreams provide us information about our problems, actions, and reactions to the previous day. If we've gotten off course somehow during the day, our dreams send us a startling image to catch our attention and get us back on track. Sometimes our dreams send us warnings about our health or things to look for in the upcoming day, but unless you understand how your particular dream images work, you may not get the messages.

Dream Ridiculus

Daffy Dream Definitions

Naked

To dream that you are naked foretells scandal and unwise engagements.

To see others naked foretells that you will be tempted by designing persons to leave the path of duty. Sickness will be no small factor against your success.

To dream that you suddenly discover your nudity, and are trying to conceal it denotes that you have sought illicit pleasure contrary to your noblest instincts and are desirous of abandoning those desires.

For a young woman to dream that she admires her nudity foretells that she will win, but not hold honest men's regard. She will win fortune by her charms.

If she thinks herself ill-formed, her reputation will be sullied by scandal. If she dreams of swimming in clear naked water, she will enjoy illicit loves, but nature will revenge herself by sickness, or loss of charms.

If she sees naked men swimming in clear water, she will have many admirers. If the water is muddy, a jealous admirer will cause ill-natured gossip about her.

Outdated definitions from a book by
Gustavas Hindman Miller,
Ten Thousand Dreams Interpreted, 1909

All dream images can be interpreted both literally and symbolically. The dream example in Lesson 1 where you heard a doorbell ringing and woke up to find someone at your door seems to have a pretty obvious meaning, so spending a great deal of time trying to go a little deeper is a little silly. But what about the dream where someone seems to be trying to suffocate you and you woke up to find the blankets over your face? At first glance, this dream would also be easy to dismiss since its meaning also seems fairly obvious. But is it? Think about your waking life. Do you feel someone or some situation might be trying to suffocate you? Or smother you? Or snuff out some of your feelings or passion?

Careful

It is also O.K. to NOT interpret a dream. I frequently have dreams that seem almost like poetry to me. I love them so much just the way they happened and find it more pleasureable just to read them over and over again. Because dreams are visual experiences, they can be wonderfully entertaining in their own right.

Just do what feels right to you in reference to your dreams. Recording them is the key to remembering them. But what you do with them beyond that is really up to you. Whatever you decide to do, have fun with your dreams.

CONSULT OTHER DREAM EXPERTS

When I first became interested in dream interpretation, I frequently used my WEBSTER'S DICTIONARY as a starting point. But many times, I needed something more than a regular dictionary definition. That's when I started looking to seeking the advice of other well-known experts in their field of knowledge.

By reviewing what experts have to say, you can develop greater flexibility and imagination when trying to figure the meaning behind a dream symbol or image.

It's also O.K. to use a dream dictionary to look up possible meanings for a particular dream image. This can sometimes help you figure out what makes the image appropriate for a particular dream. Sometimes looking up the meaning of can actually help a dreamer to remember more parts of the dream.

For animal images, try:

> ANIMAL-SPEAK and ANIMAL-WISE by Ted Andrews
>
> DICTIONARY OF SYMBOLIC AND MYTHOLOGICAL ANIMALS by J. C. Cooper
>
> MEDICINE CARDS by Jamie Sams and David Carson

For health questions, check out:

> YOU CAN HEAL YOURSELF by Louise L. Hay

For unusual dream imagery, look at:

> THE BOOK OF DREAM SYMBOLS by David Fontana
>
> DREAMING INSIGHTS by Gillian Holloway (good section on extraordinary dreams and "light treatments")
>
> SEXUAL DREAMS by Gayle Delaney
>
> CURRENT DREAMS, PAST LIVES by Denise Linn (for assistance with past life dream imagery)

Symbolic Dreams

It's usually fairly easy to figure out when a dream is symbolic. Your teeth have fallen out. You're being chased by an unknown assailant. What happens in these dreams usually doesn't have a clear parallel in your everyday world. On some level, you simply know that these dream images are happening intentionally to grab your attention, screaming out "notice me!" That's when you'll want to look at individual dream images as possible symbols for something else.

At the very least, a dream will usually mean what you think it means. Begin with your first impressions or what is obvious. If your teeth have fallen out, perhaps it IS time to think about visiting the dentist. But don't stop with the obvious. Dreams are representations, not reproductions; they do not come come to tell you what you can already consciously know or perceive. Dream images ALWAYS represent more than what they are, so the more you work with them, the more you understand.

If you're trying to figure out whether or not to interpret a dream literally or symbolically, put it to this little reality test:

➤ Is there some image in this dream that seems out of place or inappropriate?

➤ Was there a strong emotion or feeling that was exaggerated?

➤ How does this dream image apply to my waking life?

Sometimes one dream image may seem a little odd or you'll get a nagging feeling about the dream. That's how you'll know if this dream image needs further investigation or not.

Each night, most of us have dreams that are similar to dreams that other dreamers are having around the world. These are universal dream themes. How many of you have dreamt about these kinds of things? The table on the following pages describes a number of these themes.

Symbols that Change

As you grow in awareness, your ability to understand your dreams on an intuitive level will improve. But sometimes you'll have a dream image that starts to change even while you are dreaming. A friend's face might change into your mother's face, a person might become an animal, or an inanimate object will suddenly come to life. The first time this happens, you might wander, "What's that all about!"

The changing or morphing of a dream image into something else is always intentional. It happens because your attention needs to really focus on that image. You are ready to see a new dimension to the image that wasn't there before. When dream images change before your eyes, suggests:

➤ The dream image is not what it appears to be.

➤ The dream image is an aspect of yourself.

Changes in dream images may indicate you need to make some changes in your waking life. Or that these changes may signify it's time to take a look at your thoughts and beliefs. Sometimes you won't know you're ready for a change until your changing dream image gets your attention. When this happens, it is time to muster up your courage to look closely at the image and take some responsibility for making changes any indicated on a personal level.

MAKE YOUR OWN DREAM DICTIONARY

You might want to make your own dream dictionary, one that contains symbols that are unique to you. Whenever you have a dream, write down the symbols that appear. Then list the meanings that you personally assign to those symbols. A personal dream dictionary is a very powerful way to document what you are learning about dream symbols.

If possible, use a dictionary format to assemble your collection. Some people use a loose-leaf binder with alphabetical tabs. They have a separate page for each diction-ary definition where they draw pictures of the symbol. You might want to makes notes about the dates and times of the dreams in which the special symbol appeared.

If needed, you can refer to your dream dictionary each time you dream. The more you use your dream dictionary, the more insight you will gain into the symbols that have special meaning to you.

Common Themes

BEING CHASED
Usually carries a strong warning something in our waking lives is catching up to us. Chasing us implies fear of whatever is doing the chasing. We feel helplessness, powerlessness, and simply want to get away.

GOING ON A JOURNEY
Walking, driving an automobile, riding a horse, rollerskating, or traveling in a train, plane, or bus represent the dreamer's destiny or path at this time. Notice how fast you are going, if you are delayed, or who you meet along the way.

WATER
Reflects deep feelings and emotions. Notice if the water (our emotions) is calm or churning, clear and clean, or murky.

HOUSE DREAMS
Represents the Soul, with different parts of the house representing your spiritual beliefs. Various rooms represent your unique talents and gifts.

FALLING
Can be very frightening, but we usually never touch the ground because we somehow manage to wake ourselves up. Sometimes a falling dream occurs when we first fall asleep. This can be our muscles simply relaxing and the sensation incorporated into the dream.

It may also have to do with leaving our physical body when we dream. We are simply having a bad landing when we re-enter our bodies. Still others believe falling dreams are warning we have lost control of a particular situation and are "headed for a fall." If you have a falling dream, it is always worth a second look to see how the dream action relates to your waking life.

FLYING DREAMS
Many people fly in their dreams. Some do this by flapping their arms, jumping into the air, or running as fast as they can. Some interpret this as the need to rise above the present problem or situation. Others feel the dreamer needs to see things from a higher perspective. If you find yourself flying in a dream and there is no dream story or plot, you might be astral traveling.

In Dreams

BEING LOST

Can mean in your waking life you have lost your sense of direction, your motivation, or touch with your purpose in life. Feeling may correspond to a situation in your waking life. Could mean you have lost some aspect of yourself very important to you. Can also be a way of expressing feelings of uncertainty or insecurity.

APPEARING NAKED IN PUBLIC

Very often we dream we are naked, usually in front of people we don't know and they generally don't seem to notice. Sometimes people realize they are naked and feel embarrassed and try to cover up. Others are proud. Are we feeling exposed and more vulnerable about something? Or are we wanting to reveal something or show something off?

FINDING MONEY OR A LOST TREASURE

Can be a way to fulfillment a wish or a need for personal recognition in our waking life. An unfulfilled wish can originate in childhood and finding a lost treasure might indicate we are emotionally ready to take another look at what we once buried.

TAKING AN EXAM

Usually occur just before facing some challenge or test in life which requires responsibility and good performance. Reflects dreamer's anxiety about the situation. The good news—students experiencing exam dreams tend to get better grades.

SEXUAL EXPRESSION

Usually has little to do with the actual sex act, but rather learning to balance our male and female energies. Dreaming we are kissing someone of the same sex does not necessarily mean we have homosexual tendencies. Each of us have both a male and a female aspect and other people can represent qualities we aspire to.

LOOSING TEETH

Teeth are a very important part of your appearance and their loss can represent your fears of becoming unattractive. Can also symbolize you are unable to understand or "chew on" some problem. Because teeth are associated with aggression, losing teeth can mean you are reluctant to get angry or "bare your teeth."

Dreamtime Science

GLIMPSES OF THE FUTURE

Some dreams really do come true. These are typically called PRECOGNITIVE DREAMS or PREMONITIONS.

A number of people have dreamed of impending disasters, including the sinking of the Titanic in 1912 and the Japanese attack on Pearl Harbor in 1941. Because these events affected the lives of so many people, it is not unusual for them to be "picked up" by many, many dreamers. Science has no real explanation for this phenomenon, but has documented that it is real.

Precognitive dreams or premonitions result from what is called extra-sensory perception (ESP). Generally, a precognitive dream will seem very clear, almost vivid or brighter than normal. Things seem to be happening in the dream much as you would expect them to happen in real life but they seem to leave a deep impression on the dreamer's mind. The

dreamer tends to remember it, mentally going over it again and again.

Precognitive dreams are merely warnings of things that may happen if you don't take some action. They are not predictions of an unavoidable tragedy, but instead happen so we have a chance to change things for the better.

If you have a dream you think is a warning or a premonition, always consider the dream on a physical level first, especially if it concerns your health. Then consider the symbolic level. Precognitive dreams, like all significant dreams, can have several levels of meaning—physical, mental, emotional, and spiritual.

ERGO:

DREAMS ARE NOT
BOUND BY TIME!

Wet Dreams

I was hoping you wouldn't ask me too many questions about sex, but I also know that this was probably at the top of your list. Although this is not really my area of expertise, I am a parent and I'll share with you what I told my own children about this topic.

To begin with, sexuality appears regularly in the dream state. It is not unusual for men to have erections or women's vaginas to moisten while they are in REM sleep. Those physical events are a normal and natural part of the dream state.

Wet dreams happen. They are not usually about doing the wild thing. Your body is your body and sometimes it has a physical reaction to something in your dreams.

Wet dreams are a little like waking up in a cold sweat. It could be caused by something physical. Perhaps in the night your body was fighting off a cold. Your temperature was elevated because you had a slight fever and now your body is cooling off and you wake up in a cold sweat. Or you could have had a scary dream and your were running very hard and broke out into a sweat. You don't remember that dream, but you wake up in a cold sweat. It's a physical reaction.

Yes, it is possible that while you were sleeping, you dreamt of doing the wild thing and yes, you woke up wet. This does not mean something awful is going to happen or that you are a bad person, especially if you did things that you normally would not do in waking life. It simply means that you are growing up and what happened in your dream was a little like a dress rehearsal. Hopefully, the real thing will happen later—much later!

Putting It All Together

So far, you've learned about the picture language that your dreaming mind uses to create your dreams. You've also learned how to begin to understand the signs and symbols in your dreams. The magical practices will help you further with this.

The method you use to interpret your dreams is less important than the meaning you personally derive from them. Try several different dream interpretation methods because each can give you a unique pathway to understanding yourself. In time you may find one method of working with your dreams fits you better than the others.

As you begin work with your dreams, you may look at each dream as a separate news story from within. Once you have recorded a large number of dreams, you may sit back and view them over time as a collective whole. Both approaches tell you much about your real world life and reveal your hidden, magical possibilities!

Magical
Practice

One Thing Leads to Another

skills   • helps to unblock the creative imagination
developed   • thinking helps to loosen up the intuition

In this exercise, you will be learning how to use word association to take a closer look at a dream image. You write down the name of the dream image and list as many things that this word remind you of. One of your English teachers might have had you do something like this before writing a poem.

Word association exercises are meant to free up your thinking by letting your mind drift and be free. Try not to get hung up on thinking that there is a correct way of seeing what a image can mean. Go with whatever comes to mind and even branch out from one association to another so that you look at the original word in a variety of ways. When doing word associations, keep the color and the object together. A red wooden chair is different from a brown cloth-covered one. Keeping the attributes together keeps the association clear.

You might be wondering how you can determine which association is the correct one for your dream im age. In some way, any association that you come up with is correct because it is how your mind reacted to the dream image, but you're looking for the one association that sheds the most light on your dream. As you work with this exercise, you will make some meaningful connections, but you will just know that one of your associations is what the dream image means on an intuitive level.

PUTTING PIECES
TOGETHER

1. In your Dream Journal, locate the dream you recorded in Lesson 1.

As you review the dream, underline one or two dream images that you'd like more information on.

2. On a separate piece of paper, write down one of the dream images you want to take a closer look at and circle it.

3. Begin to write down the things you associate with this word.

Try to work as quickly as possible. Don't think up words. Write whatever comes to your mind without pausing.

Magical Practice

4. When you want to uncover other possible meanings for the dream image, take one of the associated words and create another list of words to go with with it, like a chain reaction.

5. As you look at your associations, you can usually find one or two ideas that feel right.

    Or you'll see an association that seems close to something you think the dream was all about. Sometimes just understanding one major image can suddenly reveal the entire meaning of the dream.

6. Write your feelings and your discoveries in your Dream Journal.

SAMPLE DREAM

As an example for this exercise I've chosen the word dollies (baby dolls) from the following dream.

I am in the house where I grew up and I am playing dollies with my friend Nancy. While playing, Nancy's face changes into my mother's and she starts bossing me around. I get angry and yell at her and she leaves. I feel calm and relieved and I wake up.

One Thing Leads to Another (cont.)

As I looked at the words a *pet project* in my sample dream, I realized that on the previous day Nancy and I were talking about a new writing project that I was trying to start. Nancy was a little tired and stressed out about her own life so she wasn't her usual supportive self as we talked about my ideas.

Maybe on some level, I felt like she blew me off a little like my mother used to do when I was a little kid.

Once I made that association, the entire meaning of the dream fell into place for me.

Magical Practice

Drawing Your Dreams

skills developed
- helps unblock creative imagination
- loosens up and develops intuition
- promotes a relaxed attitude about self-expression

We are now ready to try another method for interpreting dreams. In this one, you'll be drawing a picture of your dream after thinking about the feelings expressed it. You'll will be using color to capture your overall feelings about the dream.

Try not to worry about your artistic ability or chosing the right color. You are not trying to make a pretty picture. You are trying to get your hand to do the thinking, like being in the dream, but drawing it on paper. What you draw doesn't have to make sense or be realistic.

The picture you draw of the red chair in your dream, for example, doesn't have to look like a chair. You can draw the feeling of red with its raw power and creative energy. Or you could draw the stiffness of the red chair with its creative energy blocked or contained. What you are trying to do is free up your intuition so some of your unconscious feelings can rise to the surface.

Seeing
Feelings

- Make any preparations needed so that you will not be disturbed.

- Take several deep breaths to help yourself relax. Breathe in. Breathe out. Again. And again.

1. Pull out your crayons and markers and find a comfortable place where you can reflect on your dream.

2. In your Dream Journal, locate a dream you've already recorded, one you'd like to learn more about.

3. Read the dream description again and close your eyes and try to feel the dream images once more.

    Let you mind drift over the images of the dream without trying to analyze or interpret its meaning.

4. In your mind's eye, find the color of one of your dream images.

    Greet that image and its associated color. Continue finding the colors of your dream images until you feel like drawing.

5. When you are ready, take your paper and markers and draw your dream or anything else that comes to mind.

Magical Practice

6. When you are finished drawing, use your Dream
    Journal to write about what you felt during this
    exercise.

I am indeed a
practical dreamer...
I want to
convert my dreams into
realities as far
as possible.

Mahatma Gandhi,
Indian Statesman

SUGGESTIONS FOR PARENTS

Listen and Assist

➤ **Be honest with your teens.**

It's never easy to talk with teens about sex. But let's face it, that IS what's on their minds. Hormones are hormones and physical changes are part of growing up. I tried to explain wet dreams in an open and honest way. If you feel the need to explain it even further, please be my guest.

➤➤ **Listen, but try not to interpret or analyze your children's dreams.**

I know it's tempting and even a little fun to tell other people what you think their dreams mean. But with kids, if you try to analyze their dreams, this will shut them up quicker than anything. Simply listen to their dreams and ask them what they think their dreams mean. If you simply can't resist giving your reactions to a particular dream image, try to phrase your statements carefully with something like: "You know, if that were my dream, I might think…."

➤➤ **Create a family dream dictionary.**

Some families find it helpful to have a family dream dictionary to keep track of their commonly shared dream symbols.

Are there images or symbols that show up often among the dreams of family members? Do some members of the family share more similar symbols and images than others?

Do not be afraid to explore similarities and differences while creating this family dream dictionary.

Lesson 5

Creating Doorways to the Dream World

The car is so very hot. Mom just yelled at me when I tried to crack open the window. She says too much wind will mess up her hair. My stepfather, Jim, is driving and we've gone on another Sunday afternoon ride in the country.

Donna fell asleep not long after we got into the car and is slumped against the other rear door. Gretchen is perched between us reading a book. Bored with trying to do my Latin homework, I start to look out the window instead.

To keep my butt from falling asleep, I rearrange myself, snuggling up to the cold handle on the rear door. I look out past Gretchen's book, past Donna sleeping, and see open fields as they roll on by.

That's when I saw the two men riding on horseback. Even though they are far away, I know it's Little Joe and Hoss coming for me. My horse is trotting a little ways behind Little Joe's horse. I love my horse. She's all black except she has a white diamond on her forehead. Her name is Beauty.

In a matter of minutes, they manage to catch up with our car. Even though the window is closed, I hear Little Joe say, "Hey Katie, time for you to take Beauty for another ride." Very quietly I slip out of my seat and climb out through the rear window. Even though I'm on the trunk of the car, Jim doesn't seem to notice me. Then, without a moment of hesitation, I jump swiftly onto Beauty's bare back, and off I go!

"Riding on Beauty's Back"
daydream, August, 1963

126

We all daydream at times about things we would rather be doing. It's natural. Besides, those who tend to daydream a lot grow up with a good imagination and are more able to remember their dreams at night. Daydreams are a great place to start dream work.

When you start working with your dreams and perhaps get frustrated when you can't recall them, it is helpful to keep in mind that most people aren't able to remember their dreams. But if you're like me, you probably want a little more from your dreams. All you really want is a little help in learning how to recall your dreams with some regularity.

Once you can recall your dreams, you can learn to use them for problem solving or for exploring distant times and places. You probably already do these things and more on most nights, but if you aren't working with your dreams, you may not realize it.

Dare
To
Dream!

Reasons We Forget Our Dreams

Any number of things can interfere with dream recall, so it is not always a matter of fixing one thing. People don't remember dreams for several reasons: lack of importance attached to dream work, childhood conditioning to repress dreams, overly active lifestyle, too many outside intrusions, or a less-than-optimum sleeping environment.

LACK OF IMPORTANCE

We get from our dreams what we put into them. Most people in the United States have been raised in households that believe dreams serve no real purpose. As children, many people have also been told that dreams should not be taken seriously.

If you were told as a child that dreams have little meaning, then expecting marvelous dream recall is a little naive. But simply opening yourself up to the possibility that dreams may have meaning and be worthwhile can improve your ability to remember them.

CHILDHOOD CONDITIONING

Some people only remember the really scary dreams. Perhaps when they were small children, they had many nightmares, so began repressing all of their dreams, pushing them deep inside of to avoid reliving them. Repression is a natural defense mechanism that protects us against painful memories, fears, and even desires that we may think or were taught are unacceptable.

For many people, it's hard to escape what we are taught as young children. If you have been repressing dreams, finding a dream buddy or joining a dream study group can be very beneficial.

Overly Active Lifestyle

Some people are simply too revved up to sleep soundly enough to remember their dreams. As a kid, I was pretty wired and frequently stayed up at night, too excited to even go to sleep. As an adult, if I get overly excited about an upcoming event, I generally will not remember my dreams.

Some people spend all their energy in their waking lives and so they have no energy left over at night. If you lead an incredibly busy or extremely stressful life, you may not remember your dreams.

Outside Intrusions

Anything that significantly affects the chemistry of the body can interfere with dream recall. Even antihistamines you may take for allergies or colds can affect your sleep. Other chemicals to avoid include alcohol and drugs.

If your sleep is frequently interrupted, it will take longer to arrive at dream sleep, so there are fewer dreams to remember. If you live where there are horns blaring or phones ringing, the chances of remembering your dreams can be diminished. Falling asleep with the television on or loud music playing can also hinder your dream recall.

Dreams are also affected by the lunar cycle. Five days before a full moon, dreams begin to get stronger and clearer, peaking with the full moon energy. If you are not centered, the full moon can scatter your energy and your dreams may seem strange. Some people become depressed during a full moon cycle or experience extreme energy fluctuations.

Sleeping in the same room with another person can also interfere with dream recall. If someone is snoring or having nightmares, your sleep can be interrupted and you miss out on the much needed dreaming time.

SLEEPING ENVIRONMENT

Sometimes our sleeping environment isn't conducive to good dream recall. Take a few minutes and look around your bedroom or your current sleeping environment. Ask yourself: "Is this a place where I can relax and get a good night of sleep?"

Be truthful, now. Is your bedroom a little too messy? Is the clutter in your bedroom adding stress to your life? Clutter in our waking world can reflect clutter in our inner world. If clutter or disorganization is a problem, set this book aside and clean your room. I'll wait over there on the bookshelf until you are finished. As you bring order to the clutter in your physical world, you bring order to your inner world and can increase your ability to recall your dreams.

Sometimes the physical layout of our bedroom can also affect our dream recall. Different traditions have

𝔇ream 𝔯idiculus

Daffy Dream Definitions

Tea

To dream of that you are brewing tea foretells that you will be guilty of indiscreet actions, and will feel deeply remorseful.

To spill tea is a sign of domestic confusion and grief.

To dream that you are thirsty for tea, denotes that you will be surprised with uninvited guests.

Teacups

To dream of teacups foretells that affairs of enjoyment will be attended by you.

For a woman to break or see them broken, omens her pleasure and good fortune will be marred by a sudden trouble.

To drink wine from one foretells fortune and pleasure will be combined in the near future.

Outdated definitions from a book by
Gustavas Hindman Miller,
Ten Thousand Dreams Interpreted, 1909

different ideas as to where the head of the bed should be placed for optional dreaming. By putting the head of your bed against a north wall, you can increase stability, calmness, prosperity, and quick recuperation from illness. The north wall location is also good for increasing spiritual or magical power. The west wall is best for writers, artists, and musician. That placement can increases sensitivity for love, inspiration, and may even promote psychic ability. The bed against an east wall strengthens and sharpens mental powers. Because both the sun and moon rise in the East, sleeping from East to West can be beneficial because your body is following the natural course of the heavens.

Still others recommend that the furniture be arranged so the bed is in the middle of a circle. Circular shapes, waterfalls, candles, rainfall, and the rising moon are calming to our system and can help us to create a more peaceful and controlled sleep environment.

No matter how you arrange your bedroom, it is best if you can sleep in a pleasant place that is softly lit, quiet, and cozy. If needed, make some changes in your sleeping arrangements so you'll feel more relaxed and comfortable when you climb into bed.

When we begin to eliminate those things which interfere with our sleep and dreams, and focus on simple activities to enhance our before-bed rituals and our sleeping environment, dream magic begins to awaken.

Good Dream Recall Habits

Make an effort to remember your dreams.

Remind yourself throughout the day to remember your dreams. Even when you receive only a snippet of a dream, it is a perfect way to begin. Whatever you recall, treasure it! Be grateful and express your gratitude by saying, "Yes, this dream was perfect! Please send more!" Remember, your thoughts have power. Your mind can hear what you are thinking and it will respond with whatever you declare to be true.

Learn to relax.

Relaxation is crucial for any magic to work—even dreamtime magic. If you are stressed or worried, you may actually be keeping yourself from dreaming. Progressive relaxation and rhythmic breathing can help you remember your dreams.

Set dream goals and give yourself rewards.

Some people find it helpful to set goals for their dream work and then treat themselves to something special when they are successful. Goals could be as simple as trying to remember one dream each night or recording in your Dream Journal regularly for the next six weeks.

Work with your dream journal.

Before you go to sleep, place your Dream Journal or a pencil and some paper next to your bed. Then you'll be ready to record your dream images. Some people include extra pens or pencils. Just keeping the Dream Journal nearby reminds you to remember.

Upon awakening, be sure to hold onto your dreams.

Be gentle upon awakening. Some people find it helps to keep their eyes closed and to stay in the same position when they wake. Concentrate on the last dream of the night. Then, when you have remembered as much as you can about that dream, roll over and record it. If you can't remember any dreams, write "I didn't recall anything." But describe how you feel about the morning. Have you awakened with a sense of peace? Do you feel calm? Are you anxious or sad for some reason that you can't explain?

Improving Dream Recall

A large part of improving dream recall simply requires some attention to intending to recall your dreams and changing some of your habits. The table on the opposite page lists a number of simple things to keep in mind when you are trying to improve dream recall.

Besides considering how to change your habits a bit to help you remember your dreams, there are a number of things you can do to help open doorways to the dream world:

➤ practice with daydreams,

➤ select crystals and stones to help recall,

➤ relax with soothing bedtime rituals, and

➤ read bedtime stories.

DAYDREAMS

Daydreams are the quickest ways to create a window into the dream world and are just as real as your night dreams. Everything you've learned so far about night dreams, symbolism, and other people being reflections of yourself applies to daydreams as well. If not more so.

When it comes to daydreams, I could go on for hours, but I've talked enough. Perhaps it's been a while since you've had a really good daydream. Maybe the advice of three daydream experts can help you to remember how to do it.

Daydreams are what I do at school when I'm a little bored. I just look out the window and watch the clouds. I try to find the one that looks like a teddy bear 'cause they're my favorite thing. And when I find one, I just hold its hand and we jump up and down.

A.K., Orlando, FL, age 6

I daydream when riding the bus to school. I just sit back and zone out and let my mind drift to wherever it wants to go. In most of my daydreams, I'm hanging out with my friends, skateboarding, and doing some really amazing stunts.

D.K., Long Beach, CA, age 13

Lately, I've been daydreaming about going to college. In study hall, my mind just kind of wanders and suddenly I'm in a college classroom where I hear a professor talking. I don't know what kind of class it is, but I'm liking it because I'm learning new and different things. And then there's a really cute guy sitting next to me, but I don't want to tell you what happens next.

J. A., Dayton, OH, age 17

What each of these day dreamers intuitively knows is that they are altering their lives as they day dream. Each of them is keeping their inner magic alive. Their daydreams show imagination and creative thinking.

During an interview with D.K., I learned that he frequently thinks up new things to do while skateboarding. Then he sees himself doing the stunts in his mind's eye. Even before he tries the stunt for the first time, he has performed it in his mind at least ten times working out the kinks. In this way, D.K. uses his daydreams to perform difficult physical tasks so that he is mentally ready to do them in real life.

J.A's reaction to sharing her daydreams is fairly common. She only wanted to share what was comfortable at the time. But J.A. was also creating in her mind a dream about her future, allowing it to be as unpredictable as one that would occur during sleep. At night, J.A. was also dreaming about going to college, but her dreams seemed to be more rambling, with little direction.

By using daydreams to continue her dreams, J.A. was better able to understand some of her fears and anxieties about going to college. By going back into her daydream, she was able to practice what she needed to say or do in the future. Like D.K., she was able to try out different approaches and watch what happened if she said or did certain things. In this way, daydreams helped her solve her problems more creatively.

CRYSTALS AND STONES

Rocks, crystals, and gemstones are often used for magical purposes and can also be used to improve dream recall and for deeper exploration into the dream realm.

It is preferable to have several rocks, crystals, and gemstones you use only for dreaming. There are a number of ways you can work with crystals and gemstones:

☆ Keep your crystals or gemstones in a special place when you are not using them and wrap them in silk to hold their energy (black silk is especially good).

☆ At night, place your rocks or crystals on your night stand or table near your bed so that you can see them and admire them.

☆ Put crystals around your bedroom as a general booster to increase the energy in your sleeping environment.

All of the stones listed in the table on the opposite page will help with you with dream recall.

YOUR BEDTIME RITUALS

Falling asleep stressed and worried about the day means our bodies will have to work extra hard helping us relax. What we do before we go to sleep can limit or enhance our ability to recall our dreams, and this is particularly true of what we eat and drink. If we eat foods we have trouble digesting just before we go to bed, we are likely to have dreams that are "hard to digest." For example, I am lactose intolerant, which means I have trouble digesting diary products. If I eat pizza later in the

Stones for Improving Dream Recall

Amethyst

Excellent for improving dream recall. Balances and aligns energies during sleep. Helps the mind to go deeper into other levels of consciousness. Violet, a combination of red and blue, symbolizes the qualities of the physical and the spiritual, waking and sleeping.

Aventurine

Green-colored variety the most common. Instills a sense of balance and stability. Increases creativity. Reinforces decision-making abilities. Balances energy from hormones or the influence of the moon.

Citrine

A variety of quartz, colors range from light yellow to a golden brown to a burnt amber. Lightest color has milder effect. Very useful for slowing things down. Helps create a steady pace and a sense of stability. Very useful for calming or slowing down before going to sleep.

Herkimer Diamonds

One of best stones for remembering dreams. Protects us during dreamtime. Stimulates vibrant and memorable dream activity. With regular use, can assist astral projection and lucid dreaming.

Lapis Lazuli

Deep blue stone said to have existed before time. Opens dream doorway to ancient wisdom. Assists in developing insight into dreams. Connects with dream forces when you are in an altered state. Used to explore planetary wisdom or to connect with Mother Earth.

Moonstone

Soothing to the emotions. Colors can range from white to gray to bluish silver. Believed in many cultures to change with the phases of the moon. Since the cycles of the moon are connected to dream cycles, moonstone can connect you more deeply with your inner dream states.

Quartz Clusters

Stimulates multiple dream scenarios that are tied together. Encourages several dreams with different imagery but same dream theme. Clarifies relationships between dream images and themes. Assists with dream comprehension and interpretation.

139

day, I tend to have restless dreams and usually wake up remembering only a few rambling dream fragments.

You might want to try drinking a calming herbal tea before bedtime to help you to wind down. If you enjoy milk, try it hot with some honey in it. Milk contains nutrients which help bring on sleep. But avoid adding cocoa since all chocolate products contain caffeine. Avoid nicotine and caffeine for at least an hour before bedtime—they are both harmful to sleep. Other beverages that also contain high amounts of caffeine include most colas and soft drinks and coffee.

There are many things you can do to encourage peaceful sleep even if you are not actively working on dream recall:

☆ go to bed about the same time each day,

☆ eat a light meal in the evening and eat very little before going to sleep,

☆ clean up your bedroom or sleeping environment,

☆ spend some quiet time thinking over the day,

☆ doing some deep breathing exercises to help you relax,

☆ read a bit before going to sleep (something besides thrillers!), and

☆ listen to lullabies and soothing music.

Bedtime Stories

All bedtime stories are a product of the creative imagination and can be used to stimulate your dreams at night. The real key to opening the doorways to the dream world is to read bedtime stories with the idea of becoming one of the characters in the story. Or, if you'd like, you can become a thing or a place in the story. When you do this, you'll be practicing what is known as *sympathetic magic*, which means that what you do on one level affects you on another level.

You probably already know a little something about sympathetic magic. Think of your favorite book or favorite movie. You know, the one where you identified so heavily with the heroine that at some point in the story, you and she were one. As she struggled with villains, bad luck, and of course, love, you struggled right along with her. As she learned her lessons, you learned them too. Depending on how the story was told, you may have even known things that your heroine didn't know. Perhaps you already knew where the bad guys were hiding

Moon Water Tea

To improve dream recall, place a bowl of water outside in the moonlight for at least an hour. Be sure that the moonlight shines directly onto the water. Drink this Moon Water Tea just before going to bed and have sweet and magical dreams.

141

Soothing Music

Traditional Lullabies

Rock-a Bye-Baby   Sleep and Rest

Golden Slumbers   Day and Night

Sweet and Low   Winkum, Winkum

All the Pretty Little Horses   Twinkle, Twinkle Little Star

Other Lullabies

Reverie
by Debussy

Barcarrolle
by Offenbach

Dreams
by Wagner

Humming Chorus
by Puccini

Intermezzo
by Granados

Lullaby
by Khachaturian

None but the Lonely Heart
by Tchaikovsky

Liebestraum
by Liszt

Arab Dance
by Tchaikovsky

Dream Pantomime
by Humperdinck

Andante Cantabile
by Tchaikovsky

Evening Prayer
(from Hansel and Gretel)
by Humperdinck

Serenade
by Schubert

Lullaby
(cradle song)
by Brahms

Nocturne
by Grieg

Gymnopedie No. 1
by Satie

or where the keys to the palace could be found. What fun you had!

If it's been awhile since you've read a good children's book, take some time and visit your local library. Just wondering around the children's section can be a lovely way to spend an afternoon. If you haven't read one of the Harry Potter books, treat yourself! Harry and the other characters are great! If all of the Harry Potter books have been checked out, you might look for books by other authors who've also written a series of books with a focus on magic:

☆ *The Chronicles of Narnia* by C. S. Lewis,

☆ *The Dark is Rising Sequence* by Susan Cooper,

☆ *The Earthsea Trilogy* by Ursula K. Le Guin,

☆ *The Lord of the Rings Trilogy* by J. R. Tolkien,

☆ *The Redwall Series* by Brain Jacques, and

☆ *The Time Quintet* by Madeleine L'Engle.

Other great children's authors include: Jane Yolen, Paul Goble, John Bellairs, Eleanor Cameron, Diane Duane, Edward Eager, Diane Wynne Jones, Robin McKinley, and Philip Pullman.

The things you do to improve your overall health and your sleeping habits and environments can make a tremendous difference in your ability to recall your dreams.

Find a Dream Buddy

As you start your work with your dreams, it is very helpful to have someone you can talk to about your efforts. If you're not recalling your dreams, you can talk about what might be blocking you from doing so. If you're bothered by nightmares or recurring dreams, it is essential that you find a friend whom you can trust. This person might be able to help you sort through some of the more difficult dream images that you might encounter. This person is a dream buddy.

However, finding a dream buddy is not always an easy task. One way to look for this person is to start talking casually to people about their dreams. Most people have had at least one strange dream in their lifetime and usually they are willing to talk about it.

Listed below are the questions I ask to get people started talking about their dreams. You can use them for starters, but I encourage you to add your own questions. Try not to over analyze what others tell you about their dreams. You might want to take notes if it is O.K. with the other person. That way you will be able to remember who said what.

➤ Do you like to dream?

➤ How often do you dream?
   Nightly? At least once a week? Rarely? Not at all?

➤ Do you remember your dreams?
   Usually? Sometimes? Not at all?

➤ What is the earliest dream you can remember?

➤ Do you ever have nightmares?
   What do you do when you have a nightmare?

➤ Have you ever had a dream about the future?

➤ Are you curious about your dreams?

➤ Do you feel that dreams are important?
   If yes, tell me more…

➤ Do you want to know what your dreams are all about?

➤ Do you sometimes try to interpret your dreams?
   How often?

As you ask these questions, what you want to find is someone whose eyes seem to light up when it comes to talking about dreams. You want to find someone who says, "Oh wow! That's a great dream! Tell me more!" That way, you'll know that this person is as excited and curious about dream work as you are.

Having someone to share your dreams with will improve your dream recall. The natural place to find a dream buddy is with family or friends. In addition to writing about your dreams in a Dream Journal, take time to talk about them. Even if your talking to a pet, a doll, a stuffed animal, or youself looking into a mirror, there is something about hearing yourself describe your dreams with your own voice that makes your dreams come alive.

Dream Incubation

Another dream technique, *dream incubation*, can help us solve our problems creatively. The process of dream incubation consciously guides the course of our dreams while we are awake. It can be used at night before we go to sleep or during the day while we are awake.

Later in this lesson, there is a magical practice which describes this process in more detail. But, in general, this process involves thinking about a problem before going to sleep and then falling asleep with a question on our mind. During the night, we will generally have a dream that addresses the question we asked.

Sleeping on a problem is not a new idea. Many ancient societies believed they could use their dreams to find the cause and cure mental and physical problems. By the sixth century B.C., the Greeks made dream-seeking into a religious rite and called it dream incubation. The word incubation comes from the Latin word *incubare*, which means to lie down upon. The Greeks built special dream incubation temples and people would travel many miles to visit them.

Greek literature is filled with stories about people with problems traveling to these marvelous temples. Once there, the dream seekers would follow elaborate preparatory procedures before going to sleep. Angelic hosts or messengers of the gods would visit the dreamers. The god's messengers would deliver a special dream, offering solutions, help, comfort, or healing.

Dreamtime Science

Inventing While You Sleep

There are many famous stories of scientific breakthroughs and problems solved during sleep.

The Sewing Machine Needle

Perhaps one of the most famous of these stories is the nightmare of Elias Howe, the man who invented the sewing machine.

He had worked for weeks on his new invention, but couldn't seem to figure out how to thread the needle and still have the top of the needle attached to the sewing machine—until he dreamt cannibals captured him and as the cannibals marched around him, he saw the spear held by chief had a hole in the point.

The Benzene Molecule

Frederick August Kekulé, a German chemist, had been trying to solve a problem about the arrangement of carbon atoms in a molecule of benzene. He saw atoms juggling before his eyes and

eventually distinguish larger structures of different forms in long chains, many of them close together, and moving in a snake-like and twisting manner.

When one of the snakes got hold of its own tail and the whole structure twisted, he woke up knowing the six snakes he saw arranged in a hexagon were the six carbons in the now well-known benzine ring.

AN IMPROVED GOLF SWING

Jack Nicklaus once told a newspaper reporter he corrected his golf swing by something he learned from a dream. One night he dreamt about holding his golf club in a different manner than he usually did and he was swinging perfectly.

When he got to the course the next morning and tried to hold his club in the way he had in his dream, it worked!

ERGO:

DREAMS HELP US SOLVE
PROBLEMS CREATIVELY!

149

Even sleepers are workers and collaborators in what goes on in the universe.

Heraclitus,
Greek philosoher

The Dream World Threshold

With all these methods, you can create doorways into dreamtime, stimulating greater dream activity. When you use activities to prepare for dreamtime, you are sending a powerful message to the dream world that you are open to communication. Your actions can actually restore communication with those levels of consciousness that speak to you through your dreams.

Once dream recall begins, start writing. It also helps to write down any information received on any topic. Even the most fleeting memory of a dream is important.

Although there are many things that can interfere with remembering your dreams, there are also many things you can do to improve your dream memory. As you set the stage for your night of sleep and dreams, you will find you have opened the doors to a magical world. You will soon be filling your journal with wonderful night-time adventures!

Magical Practice

Exploring Blocks to Dream Recall

skills developed
- increases dream recall
- provides a reference point for dream work

If you've found it difficult to remember your dreams, perhaps some attitude or belief is preventing you from doing so. Some of you may already know what your family and friends think about dream work, and some of you may not. Most of us want others to accept what we are doing, so the attitude of others can keep us from recalling and talking about our dreams.

But what about your attitude? If you're like me, sometimes I don't know what I think until someone asks me a question. So, in this exercise, I'll start by presenting you with some thoughts about dreams that clients have shared with me. Until they verbalized their thoughts, they weren't aware how these thoughts were affecting their dream recall.

I'm not sure that dreams are all that important.

I don't have the time to devote to remember my dreams.

My dreams sometimes keep me up at night and
I need all the sleep I can get!

I'm afraid that if I start working with my dreams,
I'll open myself up to negative forces in the
Universe and they will invade my body.

As a kid, I had lots of nightmares and I just don't want
to start having those kinds of dreams again.

My mom has dreams that seem to come true, and
I don't want to know what the future has in store
for me.

I don't like it when there is too much sex in my
dreams. I'm not like this in real life and I feel bad
about how I'm acting in my dreams.

I've had some dreams where I've gotten very angry
with other people and I don't like seeing this side
of me. I feel worse when I wake up knowing I've
gotten so out of control!

One time I dreamt that my boyfriend broke up with
me and then, the next day he did. I was
heartbroken and I don't now if I can handle this
type of thing again.

As you look at the thoughts of others, it might help
you see where you too might be blocking your ability to
recall your dreams.

Magical Practice

EXPLORING
BLOCKS

1. In your Dream Journal, on the top of a blank page,
    write the date and the heading "My Thoughts
    About Dreams."

    Compare your list to the thoughts about dreams listed
    in the introduction to this exercise.

2. As you look at this list of comments about dreams,
    notice all of the remarks about *don't want to* or *don't
    like this*.

    When we say we don't want to do something or don't
    like to do something, we send a message to our
    subconscious that we are not ready to deal with this
    topic at this time.

3. If you've listed thoughts with the words *don't* and
    can't, try to understand that on some level you might
    not want to remember your dreams at this time in
    your life.

    Realize that you may be blocking yourself from
    remembering your dreams.

    If in your comments you find a thought that is very
    important to you and you see now that it may be
    blocking your remembering your dreams, acknowl-
    edge that it is more important to you to have this
    thought than it is to remember your dreams. Just

Exploring Blocks to Dream Recall (cont.)

don't put lots of pressure on yourself to try to remember
your dreams at this time.

4. **If you have a thought you'd like to change, then
create a new thought to replace it.**

   Make two columns in your Dream Journal and label
   one OLD THOUGHT and the other NEW THOUGHT.
   Write out the old thought.

OLD THOUGHT	NEW THOUGHT
I'm not sure that dreams have value and are are all that important to me.	My dreams are important to me.

   Then affirm your new way of thinking by writing
   your new thought down. You might want to cross out
   the old thought.

Some people write their new thoughts on index cards
and placed them on their bathroom mirror or on their
night stands. The cards serve as a visible reminder you
are trying to change an outdated way of thinking.

Eventually, if you persist in your efforts, your new
thought will replace your old thought and your attitude
about your dreams will change.

Magical Practice

Creating a Dream Doorway

skills developed
- provides a tool for promoting dream activity
- increases the depth of dream work

In this magical practice, you will be holding a small stone to your third eye area between and slightly above your eyes. Sometimes it helps to tape the stone to your forehead rather than trying to hold it. Surgical tape works best for this.

> You do not need a stone to perform this exercise. If you don't have a stone, you can just touch the third eye with a drop of clear water or sandalwood oil before going to sleep.

156

OPEN SESAME!

1. Hold a small stone to your third eye, squeezing it softly to release its energy into your auric field.

2. In your mind's eye, see your dream stone.

   Know that it will be your agent in the dream world, working to bring you the kind of dreams that you have requested.

3. As you start to fall asleep, see yourself in your mind's eye...

   You are going down a long hallway. This hallway will lead you to another hallway, then another. At some point, you will find a hallway that has a small door.

   When you see this door, know that it will lead you to the dream world. See yourself opening the door and stepping though it.

   You have now entered the mysterious realm of the dream world. See this, feel this, know that it is real.

Go to sleep. Sweet dreams!

Magical Practice

Writing About Daydreams

skills developed
- stimulates daydreaming
- increases the depth of dream work

Just like your night dreams, it's equally important to keep a record of your daydreams. For me, recording my daydreams is always a little tricky because I do my best daydreaming when I'm driving in my car or when I'm waiting for food in a restaurant. Many of my daydreams end up being recorded on the back side of napkins, placemats, or a used envelope found in my purse. I've even been so desperate, I've written on pay stubs and deposit slips!

Since daydreams play such a critical role in helping us develop our magical self, please record as many daydreams as you can. Just use whatever piece of paper you can find! And no, I have to admit that I am not so disciplined that I later record my daydreams into my Dream Journal. But I treasure my daydreams and keep my "napkin notes" in a special folder on my desk. Many of my daydreams have ended up as source material for poems, articles, stories, or letters to friends.

In this magical practice you will have an opportunity to record some of your daydreams, including the earliest daydream that you can remember. If you are currently not doing much daydreaming, then you'll want to encourage having some. Once you get going, I'm sure you'll quickly remember how much fun it is to daydream.

ONCE

UPON

A

TIME...

1. At the top of a blank page in your Dream Journal, put the date and write the title: My Daydreams.

2. Underneath the title, begin to write about the earliest daydream you can remember.

   If you had an imaginary friend as a child, write about the things that you and your friend did, how you met, the things you did, and what you learned.

3. **When you're finished writing about your past daydream, turn to a blank page and write about a recent daydream argument.**

   Talk about why the argument happened, what you did, and how the other person responded. Don't worry if you sound sarcastic or mean as you write about your daydream. Oh—and about that moment when you felt like pulling the other person's hair out in the daydream. That's pretty normal. Happens to me all the time!

   If it's been awhile since you had a daydream argument, make one up. Think about who you'd really like to get into it with. Maybe it's your second grade teacher who was a real jerk. What about your boss, your mom, or your "wicked" stepmother. The idea here is to get as wild and crazy as you can.

4. **Sit back and read what you've written again.**

   Doesn't it feel good to get this down on paper!

5. **Wait at least two days before trying to interpret your daydreams.**

   Let them mellow for a little while.

   When you're ready, you might want to try drawing a picture of your daydream and see where that leads you. Just try the same methods you use for understanding your night dreams.

Dreams guide us and help us after we set goals and ideals within our lives.

Edgar Cayce,
ARE Journal, No. 6, 1972,
p. 279

Magical Practice

Doing Homework While You Sleep

skills developed
- provides a tool for problem solving
- enhances dream activity
- increases the depth of dream work

In this magical practice, you will use the general steps most people use when they practice dream incubation or sleep on a problem. The results of sleeping on a problem depend on the amount of time you want to invest in the dream incubation process. If you try to dream about something just to see if you can, it usually won't work because you've set into motion an element of self-doubt. Also, a quick decision to incubate a dream five minutes before you hop into bed is probably not going to give you the best of results. The dream incubation process requires sincerity, concentration, patience, and persistence.

Think about a problem you want to solve. When you're struggling with an emotional issue and feel a need for help or insight, it's a good time to incubate a dream. If you are searching for a way to solve a problem that needs creativity or originality, then dream incubation can also be very effective. However, if this is your first experience with dream incubation, you might want to save the major career or major relationship decision for a later date!

SEEKING

ANSWERS

1. **Immerse yourself in the problem.**

   If your problem isn't already the primary thing on your mind, give it some thought. If at all possible, talk with other people about your problem, gaining as many different perspectives as you are comfortable with handling.

   Think about your goals. How will solving this problem change your life? What things have gotten in your way when you've tried to solve this problem in the past?

2. **Ask for assistance.**

   As you think about your situation, try to identify a specific area you want or more information on. If possible, come up with a single question that sums up what you want to know. Write this question down on a piece of paper you can slip beneath your pillow.

You can also write the question in your Dream Journal. Just remember to place it close to you so you can touch your it before you going to sleep.

3. **Before falling asleep, do something to relax.**

    Drink a cup of herbal tea, listen to some lullabies, or anything else that relaxes you before going to sleep.

4. **As you start to fall sleep, repeat your question in your mind.**

    Touch your Dream Journal or the piece of paper where you wrote your question. Know that when you awaken, you will have more information about the problem.

    Keep and open mind and be confident that you dreams will reveal information about your problem.

5. **When you awaken, do something with any information you are given.**

    Be prepared to write in your Dream Journal any dream, dream fragment, or other thought or feeling

Doing Homework While You Sleep (cont.)

that comes to you. If you need some help getting started, you might consider the following questions:

☆ What was my original question?

☆ How did this dream, dream fragment, or thought answer my question?

☆ What am I willing to do with the information given in dream?

☆ What are my next steps in response to this dream and my problem?

6. **Work with the dream in whatever way you can.**

   Do something in your waking life with the information given. This could be something as simple as changing your attitude towards another person. It may involve taking some concrete steps to mend a broken friendship in a way as simple as doing something nice for the person.

   Don't be afraid to act on the dream. When we do something positive with what the dream gives us, it opens up the flow of magic into our life.

SUGGESTIONS FOR PARENTS

Show You Care

➤ **Be a young person with them.**

With daydreams in particular, it is critical for you to realize one thing—you are the student. Throughout the day, there are many opportunities for daydreams, so rather than pulling your young people away from daydream activity, join them.

In other words, don't ask your young people if they are daydreaming—assume that they are and go there with them.

➤ **Schedule quiet time for your young persons.**

Since it is important that everyone continue to day-dream, help them by scheduling quiet time. That means no television, no radio, no friends, and no chores to do. If they want to lay on the couch and watch clouds float by, that's O.K.

➤ **Explore dream aids with your young persons.**

Some people find it helpful to place an object with a scent—a dream pillow, a bag of herbs, a sachet, a room deodorant—near their bed as a dream enhancer. The fact that you have consciously associated this scent with dreaming may trigger better dream recall.

➤ **Help kids to create bedtime rituals that create dream doorways.**

Reading bedtime stories can be a pleasant way to end the day. Stories stimulate our creativity and active imagination. You might want to suggest that your young person create a different ending to the story or put himself or herself into the story and dream on it.

➤ **Make dream sharing safe.**

If you decide to be your child's dream buddy, it is important that you be flexible with your time and attention. Your job is not to "rescue" your child, but you must be willing to listen without judgment.

➤ **Encourage kids to remember their dreams.**

Rather than asking them if they are remembering their dreams, just act as if they already do so. If you are sharing dreams as a family, simply tell them it would be nice if they had a dream or two to share with others.

Because dreams are often difficult to recall, help your children to set realistic goals about remembering them. Make sure to include rewards for dreams remembered.

➤ **Give your child time to process the events of the day.**

Another way to end the day is to quietly talk over the day's events with your children. Join them in this exercise, but try not to burden your child with your troubles. Very sensitive kids will already be worried about the happiness of their parents.

Lesson 6

Flying High
in Your Dreams

And then I found myself in an open field talking to a giant snowy owl who says to me, "You've got to let go of this thinking that you can't fly." And with those words, the snowy owl picks me up and carries me high up into the sky. We look down and see the small woods behind the house. Then we fly over some open fields and finally the snowy owl brings me back to the side yard. Rather than putting me on the ground, snowy owl takes me over to the clothesline and insists that I hang on there until I can figure out how to fly.

So there I was, hanging upside down by my toes on a clothesline not knowing exactly what to do next. That's when I started to laugh at how absurd this whole experience had become. And as I continue to laugh, my body starts to rise up and suddenly I am flying and the clothesline is flying with me. I fly higher and higher into the sky— soaring up and down, over and around, and laughing all the time. I laugh so hard I start to cough and that's when I opened my eyes.

Dream Journal
"The Day I Learned How to Fly"
May 14, 1993

Many people have flying dreams, but how they start to fly can be different. Some individuals need to flap their arms or run as fast as they can before they can take off. Other people levitate and float weightlessly above the ground.

𝔇ream 𝔕idiculus
Daffy Dream Definitions

Flying

To dream of flying high through a space denotes marital calamities.

To fly low, almost to the ground, indicates sickness and uneasy states from which the dreamer will not recover.

To fly over muddy water warns you to keep close with your private affairs, as enemies are watching to enthrall you.

To dream that you fly with black wings portends bitter disappointments. To fall while flying, signifies your downfall. If you wake while falling, you will succeed in reinstating yourself.

For a young man to dream that he is flying with white wings above green foliage, foretells advancement in business, and he will also be successful in love.

For a woman to dream of flying from one city to another and alighting on church spires, foretells she will have much to contend against in the way of false persuasions and declarations of love.

Outdated definitions from a book by
Gustavas Hindman Miller,
Ten Thousand Dreams Interpreted, 1909

Flying dreams usually contain positive emotions and in them we often feel a sense of control or a oneness with Nature. Young children frequently have flying dreams, but, as we grow older we seem to lose this special ability. Perhaps we can no longer fly once we've lost our connection to Nature. But perhaps it's something more.

Some people think that if you want to have a flying dream, all you have to do is tell yourself to fly before you fall asleep. While that may work for some individuals, flying in dreams isn't easy for most people. However, you can do many things in your waking life to open yourself up to the idea of flying in your dreams.

So what was going on in this owl dream? Did I finally lose it completely or what? Actually, this wasn't a dream, it was a spiritual journey that I experienced while attending a Shaman Retreat. Journeys are a shamanic practice used to access information from the divine or sacred part of you. During a journey, you meditate while lying down, often while listening to the accompaniment of a drum. The intent of a journey is to surrender yourself to the wisdom of your heart.

The year was 1993 and I felt like something was blocking my spiritual progress, but I wasn't sure what that something was. Although what happened in this spiritual journey was totally unexpected, it was a wonderful experience. I was thrilled to realize that I could fly once again. Even though I didn't get specific information about what was blocking me, I felt lighter, more joyful about life and knew I could now move forward.

Flight Tips

Prepare yourself for flight

Throughout the day, think about flying. Imagine you are a bird soaring through the air. In your mind's eye, see yourself flying high into the sky and viewing the world from a distant perspective.

Daydream about flying.

During the day, you can also pretend to fly in your daydreams. As you daydream, simply do the things you'd like to do if you could fly. Always remember that what we do one level can affect what happens on other levels.

Watch birds fly.

Birds are magnificent animals. Just by watching them, you bring their gift of flight into your life.

Write about your flying dreams in your Dream Journal.

On a blank page, put the date and title the page "My Flying Dreams." Then, start to write about your flying dreams. If you can only remember flying in your dreams as a child, honor that experience and write about it now. If you're not having flying dreams, write about what you would do if you could. Try to make your fantasies as real as possible. Be specific about the things you'd like to do if you could fly.

Watch flying objects.

In the man-made world, you can watch many flying objects—airplanes, hot air balloons, or kites. You can watch the movement of the sun or the moon to strengthen the idea of flight. Star gazing can be another way to rise above your daily troubles.

Astral Projection

At this time in my life I had quite of few dreams where I found myself talking with animals in remote places, such as the Alaskan wilderness or the African savanna. But nowhere in my dream journals were there any clues as to how I got there. There were no references to flapping my arms, lifting off the ground, and soaring through the air. So how did I get to these distant places?

The probable explanation is that I had astrally projected to these places. *Astral projection*, which is sometimes called an *out-of-body experience*, is considered a special state of being between sleeping and waking. When here, a person's center of attention or consciousness shifts to a place that does not coincide with the physical body.

The *astral body* relates to a second body which is said to co-exist with our physical body. The *dreaming body* is a term used in the spiritual teachings of native Americans throughout South, Central, and North America and means the same thing as astral body. This body has the same shape and appearance as the physical body, but is just energy and not solid like the physical body, so can pass through walls and objects. Yet we are just as aware of everything going on around our astral body as we are in our physical, waking body. Astral projection can happen when we are awake or when we are asleep. For most people, it happens during dreamtime. Our astral body separates from our physical body and travels on its own though time and space.

Imagine if...

- you could explore distant times and places,

- you were able to talk with a loved one who has passed away, and

- you had the ability to find out your future.

Imagine the magic!

The astral body has different names in different cultures. Ancient Britons gave it various names: *fetch*, *waft*, *tisk*, and *fye*. The ancient Greeks knew it as *eidolon* and the Romans called it *larva*. Regardless of the name for the astral body, in almost all of the written accounts of astral travel, you will find some description or reference to a silver cord being attached to the body during flight. The Asian tribes sometimes refer to this cord as a ribbon, a thread, a rainbow. African shamans call it a rope and to the natives of Borneo, it is a ladder.

Some people associate flying dreams with astral projection, but many dream experts insist flying dreams are only a forerunner to astral projection. If you are flying in a dream and then astral project, you will be able to see your physical body from outside yourself. For example, if you find yourself hovering just below the ceiling and looking down at your body and the people around you, then you are having an out-of-body experience. Or, for example, if you're sitting on top of a bookcase and staring down at yourself, then you are out of your body.

You have probably already had out-of-body experiences in your dreams, but not remembered them. Many people believe when you have a falling sensation during sleep or quick jerks, it means you have astrally projected and are just having trouble re-entering your body. There are many recorded incidents of out-of-body experiences throughout history. These descriptions are pretty much the same whether they happened in Egypt, India, South American, or even in the midwestern United States.

Characteristics of Astral Projection

When out-of-body experiences occur, there is complete mobility. Great distances can be traveled instantly. Sometimes the destination is known beforehand and this may be a foreign country where the inhabitants are unfamilar to the dreamer. Travelling to another planet, galaxy, or even in a different dimension is also possible.

On some astral journeys, it is possible to meet with spiritual beings, aliens, fairies, and gnomes. Sometimes this includes people now a part of our everyday life and sometimes those who are no longer living. For many people, encounters at this level have been known to alter their lives completely, or at the very least, give their lives an added dimension that wasn't there before.

Safety of Astral Projection

To date, I haven't been able to locate any research findings that describe an individual being hurt or damaged during an out-of-body experience. However, not everyone who experiences astral travel finds the sensation exciting or enlightening. Some dreamers who have encountered terrible extraterrestial forces with astral projection may become afraid to go to sleep.

If you have had an out-of-body experience which was unpleasant, you can place psychic protection around yourself to guard you from unwanted negative experiences during sleep and to prevent you from projecting astrally. See Lesson 8, "Dream Protection and Relaxation."

Bringing Magic into Your Dreams

In Volume I of this series, *Magic of Believing*, you learned creative imagination serves as "the key to opening the doors to the magical and spiritual realms." You can use your imagination to create changes in the world around you and to help direct the energies of your life.

In the magical practices for this lesson, you'll be using a technique called *magical daydreaming* to visualize with your mind's eye a daydream you have planned, but only loosely. You will use a *seed image*, usually something tangible in the real world such as a magic carpet, picture, animal, or character from a book, to focus your creative imagination.

You control your creative imagination, by "seeing" this image in your mind's eye. It is best if you can create this image in a three-dimensional form with as many details as you can possibly imagine. If you're like me, you'll become so absorbed within the framework of the unfolding scenario that you'll lose track of time. The ordinary world will disappear around you.

Although you will be more conscious of what you are doing during a magical daydream than a night dream, you can still learn a great deal about yourself by looking at whatever images come up for you during this process. And other images WILL come up.

Often magical daydreams will even trigger higher forms of inspiration or intuition. You may wake up from your magical daydream with a greater knowledge of your seed image, as if the seed thought had grown. The fog will clear. Some new awareness will have been created in relation to something in your daily life. You will have some new insight or understanding.

Some of you might be even inspired to write a poem or a song or even a short story in response to a magical daydream. A few of you might even want to draw or paint pictures or do a special dance to celebrate and honor your daydream experience. As you do these things, you will be making magic real within your life and adding magic to the universe.

The magical practices which follow will help you to "see with your mind's eye" by using your creative imagination—the source of your inner magic. You will be learning how to control your creative imagination, and then you can take more control of your waking life and your dreams. As you work with the knowledge gained from these magical daydreaming practices, you will come to understand that the real purpose of magic is to help you grow and evolve into your true magical self!

If you can
dream it,
you can be it
and you can do it.

Magical Practice

Going on a Magic Carpet Ride

skills developed
- develops the creative imagination
- improves the ability to communicate visual images

In this magical practice, you will be using your mind's eye and your creative imagination to fly a magic carpet anywhere in the world or the universe. Some people enjoy having an actual magic carpet that is used only for this purpose.

Magical daydreams can be a great place to begin working with improving recall, especially if you are having trouble with remembering your dreams at night.

After your magical daydream experience is over, your creative imagination will continue to work. You may experience more spiritual perceptions. In other words, once you've entertained the idea of riding a magic carpet in a daydream, it is very likely that you will be able to ride a magic carpet or "fly" in your dreams at night.

Pay attention to your dreams at night for the next several weeks. You'll want to make notes about any flying dreams or dreams in which you seemed to astral project.

To Dream Is
To Fly

- *find something to represent the magic carpet—beach towels, old blankets, or rugs work great.*

- *set the mood by playing music and lighting candles*

1. **Close your eyes and take several deep breaths to quiet your thoughts.**

    When you are ready, step onto your magic carpet, close your eyes, and visualize yourself riding it through the air.

    Ride until you come to where you want to land and visit whoever or whatever is there.

2. **When you're ready to return home, get on your magic carpet and visualize your return trip back home.**

3. **Visualize yourself bringing your magic carpet to a rest and waking up.**

After your wake up, ground yourself by breathing and stretching a little. You may want to take a drink or eat a few crackers.

As part of the grounding ritual, draw a picture of yourself and the place you visited. Take a few minutes to write about what you saw, what you did, and how you felt about the trip.

181

Magical Practice

Neptune is Calling

skills developed
- increases self-awareness
- improves our ability to control dream actions
- enhances communication with the spirit world

Many folk tales and myths begin with the story of going on a journey. In many ways, your whole life is a journey of personal growth and spiritual evolution. Everything and everyone you encounter affects the ease or dis-ease of your journey. As you move through life, you are opening to new directions and are continually building upon what you've done before.

Your personal journeys can be clear and direct or you can become lost, wandering aimlessly. If you find yourself wandering in your dreams at night, this can be a reflection of wandering around in your waking life without any real sense of direction. If you have this type of dream often, you could consider this a message that you aren't making much progress in your life. You may have developed a habit of drifting through life without any clear purpose or direction or your dreams could be tell ing you there is an unconscious wish that has not been fulfilled in your life.

In this magical exercise, you are being summoned to meet with one of the great rulers in Greek and Roman mythology. No, you're not meeting Zeus, the king of the gods, who was known as Jupiter in Roman mythology. You're meeting with one of Zeus's older brothers, Poseidon, known as Neptune by the Romans. In Roman mythology, Neptune is represented as a mature, but vigorous bearded male who is a little more sedate and little less majestic than Zeus (Jupiter). Neptune is the god of the sea and rules the unconscious and the dream world.

Mythical characters are meant to bring you into a level of consciousness that is spiritual. The magical daydream in which you meet with Neptune will be on a different level of awareness than the other magical practices you will find in this book. Neptune will bring you in touch with what is sometimes called your higher consciousness. Things that happen at a level of consciousness are very intentional. They are meant to awaken change within you.

Neptune is the representative of the divine who will talk with you about your dreams. As you speak, your conversation will tell you very personal things about your dreams. Where you are with your dreams, your successes and failures, your disappointments, and delights.

Magical Practice

The results of this magical daydream will, most likely, point out one or two areas in your life where you need to develop certain strengths or qualities. You may also be shown where you've failed to develop certain qualities in the past or failed to act successfully. You may be shown how your attitudes or beliefs are preventing you from being successful. This is sometimes very painful to see. Do not mislead yourself into thinking that transformation will be easy or a piece of cake.

The primary reason for doing this particular magical practice is so that you can learn what is hindering the full expression of your potential. You will learn more about what is blocking abundance from coming into your life at this time. Once you know this, it will be your responsibility to transform or change your life so that you can achieve the abundance your desire in your life.

Careful

This meditation needs to be approached with great seriousness, with reverence, and with a willingness to be transformed or changed by this experience.

Neptune is Calling (cont.)

THE CALL OF
THE DEEP

- *make sure you will not be disturbed*

- *set the mood by playing music and lighting candles*

1. Read the creative visualization through several times so you get the gist of what happens and can step right into the narrative.

2. Close your eyes and take a deep breath. In, out. Again, in, out, and again.

3. In your mind's eye, see yourself entering the story...

See yourself standing outside. It is twilight and you are watching the evening sky. A hint of sunlight still remains at the western rim. The air is warm and you are not quite ready to go indoors even though the shadows between the trees are deepening. Earlier in the day you had mowed the lawn so the air is rich with the smell of freshly cut grass and the excitement of the day is still with you.

Instead of going inside, you decide to lay down on the grass and watch the stars come out. It is then that the physicalness of the day catches up with you. You start to breath deeply, sighing, breathing in, then out. As you lay on the grass quietly breathing, you realize how thankful you are now for this

Magical Practice

moment and for the ability to lie down like a child on the grass and to look up into the sky in total wonderment. For a brief moment, you think about all the people in the world, children mostly, who like you are looking up into the night sky. You wonder what they are thinking about.

As you watch the first star appear, you make a wish, feeling for the first time in a long time like a child of the universe. You watch as the stars come out one by one in the evening sky, and one star in particular catches your attention. The star's glow is steady and you think to yourself that it might actually be a planet rather than a star. But you're not sure. Then you laugh at how serious you have become and think to yourself, "what difference does it make—it's just a star."

You move your head slightly to the right and your attention turns to the other stars that are coming out. Again, you feel a deep connection to Mother Earth and all her creatures. You close your eyes and continue to breath heavily, almost falling asleep.

The sound of a hoot owl awakens you. As you open your eyes, the star that you thought was a planet is right before your eyes. It is burning with even brighter intensity than before. Almost as if it is beckoning you.

You laugh and say to the little star, "O.K., you win. Come get me if you can!" and you barely finish those words when you realize the star is moving closer to you. Within a matter of minutes, you can touch it!

Neptune is Calling (cont.)

And as you touch the star, you again hear the hoot owl calling. You turn your head towards the place where the owl's sound was coming from. Then you realize you are high above Earth and looking down at yourself lying on the ground. As you look at yourself, you realize how very, very small you really are. You look like a small speck, only about the size of a very large raisin, and growing smaller by the second.

"Come with me," a voice whispers in your ear, "Neptune wants to speak with you ...."

Find the next image and let your mind float to it. Use your imagination to continue the story, floating from one image to the next until you "wake up."

Breathe deeply, and begin to stretch. Take a drink or eat a few crackers to help ground yourself and your feelings. Use your Dream Journal to write about what you felt while doing this magical daydream exercise. Write about the images that came up for you. If you asked any questions, record the answers you received.

Pay attention to your dreams at night for the next several weeks. You'll want to make notes about any flying dreams or dreams in which you astral projected.

SUGGESTIONS FOR PARENTS

Play More Often

➤ **Share your unusual dream story.**

Talk about the dreams you've had where you have flown or traveled outside your body.

If you can't remember flying in a dream, talk about where you would go and what you would do if you could fly in your dreams.

➤ **Ask your young persons to stretch their imaginations.**

Whenever you and your young person are finished reading a story, watching a television show, or coming home from the movies, ask your children what they would have done differently. If your children are hesitant, go first and really let your imagination go.

Encourage your young person to re-write endings or make changes in the major characters.

➤ **Take a magic carpet ride together as a family.**

Consider making this a special regular event in your family and celebrate the occasion.

➤ **Listen to classical music with your young person.**

Both of you close your eyes and take turns talking about where the music takes you or what the music makes you see. Describe as vividly as possible.

For example, "Ladies dressed in long, flowing gowns strolling along garden paths" or "a sunny day with horses trotting around a race track" or "pirates boarding a ship and looking for treasure chests." This can strengthen your own imagination and visualization and even make dreams more vibrant.

➤ **Allow the mystery to linger.**

Try not to feel like you need to know all the answers. When young people ask if something is true or possible, don't give them definitive answers. Encourage them to think in possibilities.

Provide them with an open-minded viewpoint that includes different levels of understanding and different interpretations of experiences.

Lesson 7

Fighting the Monsters Under the Bed

A big, black, monstrous dog was blocking the front door to my house. It was barking insistently and baring its teeth at me. Suddenly, a voice behind me says, "He looks mean, but if you want, I'll show you how to tame him."

Dream Journal
September 21, 1986

No matter if you're 5, 15, or 50, you can have scary dreams. If you've ever awakened during a nightmare, you can remember it very clearly. Even after you wake up, the terror can still remain and on some deep level, you feel like something horrible is about to happen.

At least two-thirds of all adults have had at least one nightmare in their adult lives and certain types of people tend to have more nightmares than others. So let's take a closer look at the things that go bump in the night.

Nightmares are those very scary dreams where you feel helpless in the face of unknown danger. You're frightened and want to run away, but your legs won't move. You want to scream, but when you open your mouth, no sound comes out. Sound familiar?

191

Two Types of Nightmares

Typically, nightmares come in two varieties, those occurring before midnight and those that come in the wee hours of the morning. Nightmares before midnight may be PHYSIOLOGICAL in nature when there is no emotional tension, fear, or worry. There is little truth in the old wives tale that eating certain foods such as cheese will give you a nightmare. However, if you eat a heavy

---

Dream Ridiculus

Daffy Dream Definitions

Monster

To dream of being pursued by a monster denotes that sorrow and misfortune hold prominent places in your immediate future.

To slay a monster, denotes that you will successfully cope with enemies and rise to eminent positions.

Outdated definitions from a book by
Gustavas Hindman Miller,
Ten Thousand Dreams Interpreted, 1909

meal with lots of cheese, you may suffer from indigestion and that will tend to disturb your sleep.

On the other hand, nightmares occurring after midnight tend to result more from your EMOTIONAL reactions, whether tension, fears, or worries. Even though the cause may be emotion, your body will also have a physical response to these dreams. Your heart may still pounds rapidly and you could wake up in a cold sweat.

PHYSIOLOGICAL CAUSES

Nightmares occurring in the earlier part of the evening tend to arise from pain, discomfort, and fevers. For example, if a knife-like pain is present, your dreaming self may turn the physical pain into the experience of being stabbed over and over again. This scene gives the dream a symbolic picture of a painful symptom.

When you have a high temperature, you may form dream hallucinations in which you find yourself in a frightening and unfamiliar world. Hormonal changes cause an imbalance in the body's chemistry which may produce heart palpitations, night sweats, and feelings of suffocation. These physical symptoms can be incorporated into dream images that become nightmares.

EMOTIONAL CAUSES

Nightmares can also be a response to something that has happened during the day that has frightened you or made you feel anxious. In your dreams, this anxiety or fear can become a personal attack, being chased, drowning, or some other very unpleasant ordeal.

The most common nightmare women report are ones in which they are being chased or attacked and their family can't help them. More women than men tend to report nightmares involving a threat of death to a loved one, and quite often that loved one is a parent or sometimes a peer.

Young children and teens are very sensitive to their home environment. Because of this often unrecognized psychic link to the energies of both parents, children can sometimes pick up on disharmony in the household. Even when great care is taken to shield children from unpleasantness, on some level they can often sense the disharmony and their struggle with it may come out as nightmares.

Protection During Sleep

dream-catcher

There are also several things you can do in the physical world to help with nightmares. We can borrow from Native Americans traditions and use dream shields, decorating them with personal or family objects for our protection during sleep. We can also use dream catchers to catch the nightmares so they won't filter down to us when we sleep.

In Lesson 5, we talked about crystals, stones, and rocks which can help open the doorway to the dream world and encourage dream recall. These can also be extremely effective when working with nightmares, but substitute black tourmaline, daphnite, flint, gold, and nepheline to help protect you from nightmares.

Herbs effective for nightmares include anise, cedar, huckleberry, mistletoe, morning glory, purslane, rose, rosemary, and thyme. Just having the plants or the fragrances of the plants in your bedroom will help you sleep better with less nightmares.

The Message in Nightmares

Nightmares and anxiety dreams usually serve as a warning to attend to something in our waking life. During your day you may not even be consciously aware of many of the things that frighten or threaten you, so at night your dreams serve as an emotional barometer, helping you to remember. They are meant to thump you on your head and get your attention about some situation that is causing problems, something you may actually on some level be trying very hard to ignore.

Nightmares are named after Rhiannon, a legendary Celtic Goddess of Birds and Horses. Rhiannon rode a swift white horse and was the legendary Mare-Demeter, who with her two sisters ran wild. There are stories of how Rhiannon devoured her son Hippasus (a foal). At one time, people believed that during a nightmare the dreamer's soul was abducted to the mare's nest, a terrible place that was littered with the jaw-bones and entrails of poets.

In our waking life, there are many people who have a way of manipulating us in subtle ways we may or may not be aware of, yet we are strongly affected emotionally by these things. Almost all authority figures—our parents, teachers, and bosses—can put us in a position where we sometimes feel obligated to do something we really don't want to do. Friends can even make us feel like we need to do something when we know inside ourselves this is not in our best interest. Very often we will have a nightmare when we are being manipulated to do things we don't want to in our waking life.

Nightmares provide us with a powerful learning opportunity because they can show us where a fear has been blown way out of proportion. They also point out situations where others are not treating us properly. Nightmares show us things we have repressed or stuffed inside us that are still affecting us in a negative way on some level.

Common Nightmare Themes

The most frequently reported nightmare is being chased, but another common nightmare theme is being physically attacked.

BEING CHASED OR CHASING

I'm walking alone on a deserted country road. I know someone is following me, but when I turn to look, I can't see anyone. Yet I can hear footsteps and heavy breathing. I walk faster, and the footsteps behind me speed up, getting closer and closer. I start to run, but I seem to be moving in slow motion. Suddenly I feel a hand on my shoulder. I try to scream, but no sound comes.

In these nightmares you usually feel very frightened and helpless and may be unable to move. People will report differing versions of being chased, but the dreams usually have two common elements: awareness of a threat and an inability to move.

Somewhere in a nightmare like this, you will become aware that a person or thing is out to harm you. When this happens, you will try to get away, usually by running. Often at some point, you find you can no longer move. In effect, you are paralyzed. This might be because you are subliminally aware of the loss of muscle tone which accompanies dreaming. But this can also be related to a more primal fear of being helpless in the face of danger, like a deer trapped in the headlights of an approaching car.

BEING PHYSICALLY ATTACKED

The monster is standing at the foot of my bed. Its ugly face is so horrible that I can hardly look at it. I try to hide, but my head seems to be stuck to my pillow so I can't get up. The monster just laughs at me and with red eyes glaring, it jumps on top of me and climbs inside my mouth, worming its way deep down into my body.

Being physically attacked is another common nightmare. Our attacker can take many forms: a dark shadowy figure, often a male, a ferocious animal, a demon, a monster, a mythological beast, or a fictional character. Attack dreams may come from situations in real life where we unconsciously sense some type of threat.

Taming the Monsters

The monsters and demons that appear in our dreams can have many different meanings. Sometimes we have nightmares for physical reasons, but most psychologists tend to believe that dream monsters are aspects of our personality. According to Carl Jung, a psychiatrist and dream theorist, our dream monsters can represent our enemies. Jung identified two types of enemies our monster images can represent:

➤ those that are outside of us (our enemies), and

➤ those that are inside us (our shadow self).

Whether our monsters are from the outside or from within us, each monster has its own needs and tries to get our attention. Our monster dreams can give us a good opportunity to meet and talk with different aspects of ourselves.

Nightmares and monster dreams happen for a reason. Unfortunately, because we tend to focus on the fears our nightmares produce—which is very natural to do—we sometimes forget to look for their very special message.

Common Fears

- public speaking
- being alone
- open wounds, blood
- making mistakes
- darkness
- police
- failure
- dentists
- dogs
- disapproval
- injections
- spiders
- rejection
- hospitals
- deformed people
- angry people
- taking tests

With school violence on the rise, teens, older and younger children also fear:

- being attacked, injured, or killed
- seeing friends being injured or killed
- crowds
- drug use
- gossip
- parents getting a divorce
- car or plane crashes
- being rejected in sexual relations
- school violence (terrorism)
- war
- being misunderstood

In her book, *Feel the Fear and Do It Anyway,* Susan Jeffers explains that in American society, fear has reached an epidemic proportion. Not only do we fear beginnings, but also endings. We don't want things to change, but we are afraid we might get stuck.[2]

Teen years are difficult and certain fears are just part of growing up and being in school. Many young peo;le are afraid of taking tests. Some are afraid of being misunderstood by their families or friends. Some are afraid around people who are different. The number-one fear of most adults, teens, and older children is fear of public speaking, but the list or common fears is long. Most people share some of the common fears shown in the table on the previous page. And any fear or pressure can influence our dreams.

Researchers distinguish between fluid and fixed fears. A *fluid* fear is one that comes and goes. If the fear changes from week to week or remains for a limited period and then begins to fade away, it can be considered normal. On the other hand, a fixed fear is one that remains or may even intensify. Fixed fears may require more patience to work through. If a *fixed* fear persists, you may need to enlist the help of a professional in dealing with it.[3]

---

[2]Susan Jeffers, Ph.D., *Feel the Fear and Do It Anyway,* (New York, NY: Fawcett Columbine, 1987), p. 3.

Monster dreams are wake-up calls, alerting us to the fact that we need to change our way of thinking. True magic requires a different way of looking at life. It requires that we think in new and creative ways about everything, including our dreams.

Remember too that some dreams, including nightmares, can be housecleaning dreams. Sometimes just facing the monster or the fear is all that is necessary to make it go away. At other times, we may have to do a little more work.

Dreams are wonderful and exciting adventures. That's the magic of them. As we work with them, we become more empowered. We are able to handle all situations and people within our waking life more effectively. We become more creative. We even handle the monsters of our life more easily. The magic flows from the dreamworld and comes to life more strongly within our waking world.

---

[3]Deb Gebeke. *Children and Fear,* (Fargo, NY: North Dakota State University Extension Service, November 1993), p. 1.

Dreamtime Science

PROBLEM SOLVERS AND NIGHTMARES

People who are natural problem-solvers have fewer nightmares.[4] Nightmares are lessons in problem solving and since these people work at problem-solving in their waking life, their dreams tend to be a little more peaceful.

An in-depth study conducted by Dr. Ernest Hartman, a psychiatrist at Tufts University School of Medicine in Boston, showed that certain personality types have more nightmares than others. People who are more open, vulnerable, or sensitive in nature may tend to have more nightmares. However, once these people can determine the theme or pattern of their nightmares,

---

[4]Wilda B. Tanner, *The Mystical Magical Marvelous World of Dreams*, (Tahlequah, OK: Sparrow Hawk Press, 1988), p. 251.

it is easier for them to work through the problem in their waking lives.

> If we learn to solve problems better, do we lessen
> nightmares?

> And if so, how can we do this?

Doing something as simple as solving
puzzles, doing crosswords, or com-pleting
mazes before going to bed may actually lessen
the nightmares. In MAGIC OF BELIEVING (VOL. I in
this series), we learned that one of the rules of
magic is that what we think, do, and believe
on one level affects us on other levels.

ERGO:

SOLVING PROBLEMS
IN OUR WAKING LIFE
LAYS THE GROUNDWORK
FOR SOLVING PROBLEMS
IN OUR DREAMING LIFE.

My Greatest Fears

skills developed
- eases feelings of helplessness
- provides a reference point for future dream work

One of the major problems with nightmares is that we feel victimized by our fears, especially if we don't talk about them. We need to take a close look at our waking life to determine what is making us feel fearful, apprehensive, afraid, or anxious. Once we've identified our fears, we can work on taming the monsters under the bed.

In this magical practice, you'll make a list of the fears you are currently experiencing and any fears you once had but have now overcome. Then you'll write about your nightmares. Sometimes, just by writing about nightmares, you can gain some insight as to why they might be happening.

FACING OUR FEARS

1. **At the top of a blank page in your Dream Journal, write the title "Dragons That I Have Slain."**

   Make a list of the fears you once had but have now overcome. If you cannot remember some of your fears as a young child, ask your parents about them. Many two-year-olds are afraid of being abandoned. They're also afraid of the dark, a bath, thunder and lightning, toilet training, strangers, or loud noises.

   These may seem childish now, but when you were younger, these were the dragons you had to overcome. Celebrate!

2. **At the top of another blank page, write the date and the title "My Greatest Fears."**

   List what you consider your major fears at this time. If needed, review the list of common fears in the table on page 199 in this lesson.

Magical Practice

Beside each entry, make a few notes about how long you've had this fear, whether it comes or goes, or when it seems to bother you the most. Write anything here that you think might help you understand the meaning of this fear.

Sometimes by writing about our fears you will discover they aren't all that frightening after all.

3. **At the top of another blank page, write the title "My Worst Nightmare."**

Now write about a dream you don't feel good about at all or about your worst nightmare. Dreams are not always about good things. Dreams are about the whole of life, the balance of light and darkness, good and bad.

It is important to honor and accept your nightmares as part of yourself. Every nightmare contains a gift, a message for you. As you write about your nightmare, thank it for coming into your life and giving you an opportunity to see and understand the need to make some changes.

Dreams show us how
to find meaning in
our lives,
how to fulfill our own
destiny,
how to realize
the greater potential of
life within us.

Marie-Louise von Franz

Magical Practice

Dream Champions

skills developed
- increases self-confidence
- promotes creative imagination

About ten years ago, a group of us who were studying spirituality decided to enlist the assistance of "dream champions" to help with our dream work. These are people (real or imaginary) who will fight our dream battles for us until we are strong enough to fight the monsters on our own.

One of the women in the group chose Indiana Jones to be her dream champion because "he'd know what to do to protect me." Besides, she felt Harrison Ford was very good looking and perhaps, even if she didn't have a nightmare, well, maybe Harrison could just drop by and wait with her until the monsters appeared.

I chose Keres, the guard dogs of the House of Hades or the Underworld. In Greek mythology, Hades is the mysterious, terrifying God of Death. Now, you may think this was a bit particular, but when I was eight years old I almost died and had a near-death experience. Only in the mid 1950s, no one called it that. My family refers to it as the time that I "passed out and went to Heaven and saw Grandma Shires and Uncle Sylvester (who had died several years before)."

Believe me when I tell you that I was just as shocked to see them as they were to see me. Well, Uncle Sylvester took one look at me and said "There's got to be some sort of mistake. You are not supposed to be here. You are entirely too young to die." And Whoosh! I was back in my body in no time. No dying for me that day. But from what I can remember, there weren't many animals in Heaven. Of course, I wasn't there very long and I only got to see one room.

So, for my dream champion, I wanted to borrow Keres, the God of Death's dog. That way, if death was coming my way again, I figured Keres would start to bark because he'd be happy to see his master. After all, if my friend got to have Indiana Jones as her dream champion, then I was going to get a puppy. Not that Keres is a very friendly dog, but that's another story.

My point of telling you this is so that you will have some fun when picking out a dream champion or even a team of them. You want them more powerful than you because they are going to fight the monsters for you.

Confronting your dream monsters is sometimes easier said than done. However, you don't have to go it alone when you confront your demons. A dream champion can be anyone you want: a parent, a real-life hero (perhaps a football star or a heavy weight champion), a fictional character, a friend, or a guardian angel.

Magical Practice

CALLING ON YOUR CHAMPIONS

1. **Use a daydream or a brainstorm ing session to talk with your dream champion about how to go about fighting the monsters.**

   It's O.K. to have a team of champions with different strengths to fight your monsters.

2. **Visualize your dream champions in as much detail as possible and think of possible names.**

   Choose one of your fears from the previous exercise and decide on which dream champions you will use to help fight the monster. In your Dream Journal, write a note to your dream champion asking for help. Be specific and state exactly what you want to happen.

   Dear Keres,

   Having a little trouble with my boss. Last night, she looked like a smelly old man who kept trying to smother me with a pillow.

   I know she doesn't like it when I say what I think at work. If she comes around tonight, would you bite her in the behind? Bite her hard so she gets the message. I really don't want her to come around here any more.

   Thanks and much love to you!

Dream Champions (cont.)

3. **Make a battle plan.**

   Use creative visualization to make up some dreams in which your dream champion is more powerful than the monster and together you overcome it.

4. **Celebrate your victory with your dream champion. Reward yourself with something.**

   Treat yourself to an ice cream or just do something fun for yourself. (And don't forget to thank your dream champion for the help.)

VARIATIONS: OTHER BATTLE PLANS

In addition to enlisting the help of a dream champion and having conversations with the monsters, there are several other things you can do to tame the monsters under the bed.

1. Draw pictures of your monsters. Put them in jail. Color your monsters with soft pastel colors to lessen their power.

   Remember that what we do on one level always effects us on other levels.

2. If you can figure out the problem or fear this monster represents, daydream about correcting the situation.

3. Act out the dream scene where your champion helps you win the battle.

Magical Practice

My Monster's Gift

skills developed
- promotes self-awareness
- increases creative imagination
- reveals unexplored talents

Another good technique for getting rid of your dream monsters is to meet with them face-to-face and ask them for the gift that they have for you. This works best if you can pick out the major nightmare image in one of your scary dreams and ask it to explain itself.

You will be taking the role of your nightmare image and in an imaginary conversational manner, answering your own questions when you ask your dream the image about its gift. By doing this magical exercise, you will be forced to articulate feelings about what a dream image represents. When working with nightmares this is even more effective than just reflecting and writing about monsters in dream journals.

The few times I've used this method with clients, the results have been spontaneous and immediate. When the person really gets into this exchange, the results are magical! Try this method if you've been stumped about the reasons for a disturbing dream.

If at all possible, tape record yourself as you do this exercise. That way you can hear how the different dream images talk and you'll also be able to hear how you interact with them.

It's A Surprise

- *make sure you will not be disturbed*

- *set the mood with candles, fragrances, relaxing music*

1. Choose a recent disturbing dream, preferably one with dream images which are fairly easy to recall.

2. Run through the dream in your mind to determine which image you want to talk to.

   Some people find it helpful to draw the dream image or to cut out pictures from magazines that resemble it.

3. Write down the questions you want to ask your dream image before you begin the creative visualization.

Magical Practice

4. Sit comfortably in a chair and take a deep breath. In, out. Breath again, in, out. Again, in, out.

    When you are relaxed, close your eyes and visualize in your mind the dream image appearing before you.

    Face this image and ask out loud an open-ended question about what it wants, what it represents, what it's trying to show you.

    > Who are you?
    >
    > What do you want?
    >
    > What made me dream of you?
    >
    > Why are you in my dream?
    >
    > What are you trying to show me or teach me?

5. Continue to ask questions until you have covered all the things you wanted information about.

    Don't worry about recording the answers or writing them down. You will remember them and at the end you will be able to record them in your dream journal.

6. When you are finished asking questions, visualize the dream image answering your questions.

    Trust what you imagine this monster tells you. Rely on your creative imagination to supply you with the right answer.

My Monster's Gift (cont.)

Ground your energy. Stretch a little. Eat a few crackers. Say a few words to affirm what has just happened. This can be a prayer of thanks for what already is.

Write in your Dream Journal any insights you gained about any of the disturbing dream images. Add notes about how you felt during, and after, this exercise.

VARIATION

Make preparations as you did before. As you relax and close your eyes, see yourself as the dream image. Imagine you are this "monster." Become the dream image and answer the question out loud.

Rely on your creative imagination to supply you with the right answer.

SUGGESTIONS FOR PARENTS

Meet the Monsters Halfway

➤ **Do not wake a child who is having a nightmare.**

Although it is tempting to wake up a nightmare victim to save the person from the bad dream, try not to do this. If the person sleeps right through a nightmare, chances are the person will not remember it. But if you wake someone up during a nightmare, the bad feelings from the dream may stay with the person for much of the day.

➤ **Review your own lifestyle.**

Even when great effort is made to hide disharmony from the children, children can sense it on some level. They have an often unrecognized psychic link to the energies of both parents, and if there is tension in the home, they are likely to pick up on it and have nightmares about it.

➤ **Share your own nightmares with them.**

Very often children have horrible dreams but are sometimes hesitant to share them. Depending upon their age, they may or may not be comfortable talking about dreams that frighten them, especially if there is a push for them to be acting in a more grown-up fashion.

Set an example and start talking about the first time you had a nightmare when you were a child. How old were you? Who did you tell? What did someone say or do that helped you get beyond the nightmare? This simple act of sharing your nightmare story can help a frightened or anxious child to open up.

➤ **Help fight the monsters under the bed.**

If your child is under ten, you might want to create a bedroom inspection checklist you and your child can use to search for any monsters. Make a game of creating this Monster Map. Be sure to add your child's secret hiding places because that's where the monsters will be.

At night, go over the checklist with your child seeking out the monsters! When you find them, do whatever is necessary to chase them away. As you tuck your child in bed, remember to reassure your child. You are letting your young person know that they do not have to face monsters alone.

➤ **Help your child learn how to find their dream champions.**

We all need heroes. Talk openly with your kids about who your heroes or heroines were when you were their age. Don't worry if you didn't look up to Albert Einstein or some other great thinker. When I was a teenager, I was a fan of Rocky and Bullwinkle. With those zany cartoon characters, I could easily win any battle!

Be honest with your kids. If you didn't have heroes as a young person, tell them who would you call on NOW to be your dream.

Lesson 8

Precautions and Protections

And then there I was, in a dark hallway where the air is moist and smells a little like damp earth. There are pieces of a shattered glass mirror everywhere. A voice behind me says, "And so Alice, what will you do now?"

"Alice?" I whispered the name. "You mean I'm Alice!"

"Well certainly!" the voice responds. From the tone of his voice, I know that he is slightly irritated with me. "Isn't that was this is all about? Didn't you say that you wanted to write about the looking glass. That's why I brought you here."

"Oh," I said softly, knowing full well that I must have dozed off when I was reading Alice in Wonderland. Somehow I must be talking to one of the characters in that book. "But the mirror is broken. I don't remember them breaking any mirrors."

"Perhaps not. But that was then and this is now." That caught me off guard and, for the life of me, I couldn't figure out what to say next. I waited for a long time, but the voice had nothing more to say.

Dream Journal
"Alice and the Broken Mirrors"
November 19, 1993

This dream woke me up out of a deep sleep. I had no idea of its significance. But I felt very excited for some reason because I had "connected" with Alice. Well, O.K., it wasn't exactly a connection. I was she, so she must be me, or at least that's what I thought at the time. You know how fuzzy things can get when we contemplate our dreams.

Laying in my bed, I felt around for pieces of shattered glass. The dream seemed so real that I thought perhaps one or two glass fragments might have traveled back with me. Once I knew there wasn't any broken glass, I felt it was safe to grab my Dream Journal and that's when I remembered that old wives tale:

Break a mirror and you'll have seven years of bad luck.

So, I laid there for a little while longer, trying to figure out if breaking mirrors and bad luck applies in our dreams as well as in waking life. But to tell you the truth, I couldn't figure out which one of us broke the mirror. Did I, as Alice, break the mirror or was it me, as me, who had done it. Seemed like no matter how I thought about it, I guessed "I" did it. But for some odd reason, I didn't think I had anything to do with the broken mirror so I ended what I wrote with:

T'was a puzzlement!

That way, when I came back to my dream, I would know I didn't have a clue as to what it all meant.

All that day and for several days after, I carried my Dream Journal with me everywhere. After all, I couldn't let it out of my sight since it contained this wonderful new mystery that had just been added to my life!

Dreamtime Protection

During sleep, our sensitivity increases and the possibilities of our being affected by outside influences such as a noise, emanations from an object, an entity, or the atmosphere, are intensified. Many old inns in Britain advertise their haunted rooms and many people who sleep in them have unpleasant experiences such as a suffocating sensation or feelings of impending danger.

Before this century, nocturnal attacks of a psychic nature were well recognized and acknowledged. Most people in earlier times readily understood that we needed to protect ourselves against this type of experience. Today, it is rare to see signs of dream protection in most people's homes; however, the need for protection during sleep has not disappeared.

There are a number of simple tools for dreamtime protection. Having a dreamtime mirror is one. Dreamcatchers are another and I strongly encourage you to place one above your bed. You may also want to develop a ritual for asking for divine protection while you sleep. A simple prayer that includes a request for protection is all that is needed. These three tools may seem simple, but they are some of the best for sleep and dream protection.

MIRRORS FOR GOOD LUCK AND PROTECTION

Having a mirror in your bedroom is considered good luck. You will need a real mirror for this, one with a silver back rather than aluminum. If possible, place your

---

𝕯ream 𝕽idiculus

Daffy Dream Definitions

Mirror

To dream of seeing yourself in a mirror denotes that you will meet many discouraging issues, and sickness will cause you distress and loss in fortune.

To see others in a mirror denotes that others will act unfairly towards you to promote their own interests.

To see animals in a mirror denote disappointment and loss in fortune.

For a young woman to break a mirror foretells unfortunate friendships and an unhappy marriage. To see her lover in a mirror looking pale and careworn, denotes death or a broken engagement. If he seems happy, a slight estrangement will arise, but it will be of short duration.

Outdated definitions from a book by
Gustavas Hindman Miller,
Ten Thousand Dreams Interpreted, 1909

mirror in your bedroom so it faces South. This will keep away nightmares and other nocturnal discomfort.

Mirrors have been used for over 2000 years in magical traditions. They banish negativity by allowing the bad energy to escape through them. On the Dream Shaman website, you can find a ritual for the transmuting (changing) of negative energy into positive energy.[1] You might use this ritual if you are having trouble falling asleep because you can't stop thinking about the previous day's events.

1. Stand in front of your mirror or hold a small, silver-backed mirror in your hand.

2. Bring whatever negative thoughts you have into your mind and concentrate on them.

3. Send your negative thoughts and worries into the mirror.

    After you've done this, the energy that will flow back to you will be positive.

The mirror filters the negative energy, changing it from negative to positive. In this way, you can have energy working with you rather than against you.

---

[1] The Dream Shaman, "A List of Dream Customs and Superstitions (Part I). *Electric Dreams* (June 1994), vol. 1, no. 8. Dreamgate (29 November 2000), <http://upgrad.unsw.edu.au/~mettw/edreams/articles/superstitions.html>

Dream Shields and Dream Catchers

Native Americans in North America create personal objects to cultivate inner power and strength. Very often they create an individual dream shield for assistance in experiencing the ancient mysteries. The symbols placed upon the shield relate to their family mythology

a variety of
dreamcatchers

and their personal identity. They use their dream shield to remain in alignment with their life's purpose. These shields are hung in the sleeping area for protection.

Dreamcatchers, hoops crisscrossed with webbing, can also be used for protection. The Ojibwa people believe the night air is filled with dreams, both good and bad. A dreamcatcher hung above the bed will catch the bad dreams and let only the good ones through and down the feathers that adorn it and into the sleep of the individual. When the morning sun hits the dreamcatcher, the bad dreams will disappear.

Prayer Cloths and Crosses

In England, the Victorians used prayers to call upon the Lord to bless their houses. These prayers were often embroidered into a cross-stitch design and hung above their headboards. It could be as simple as a cross-stitched sampler with a prayer or even a cloth that was used in a personal altar. Those who followed Christian traditions placed pictures of Jesus and crucifixes in bedrooms or places where people might nap. They all provide protection and peace during sleep.

Dream Sharing

I hope that by now you've been able to find someone to share your dreams with. Exploring dreams is such fun that it is only natural you might want to share what you are learning with others.

In the beginning, it is sometimes best not to talk too openly about your dreams or what you're working on. If you mention you are exploring dreams, other people will naturally want to share theirs with you. This can be a great way to learn more about the other person, but try not to analyze or interpret the other person's dreams for them. Simply listen and ask them questions and help them understand how they can learn more about their dreams. Sharing troublesome or frightening dreams is best done with a friend you can trust.

If others persist and ask you what you think their dream means, keep it simple. Respond to them in the same way you would want them to respond to your dreams. Treat their dreams kindly. Trust that you will know what to say and how to say it. If you don't have a clue as to what a dream image might mean, it's O.K. to say that. Just don't tell other people their dreams are weird or crazy. That type of feedback can be harmful to the other person. The table opposite thjs page lists several things to keep in mind when sharing your dreams.

Code for those Sharing Dreams

➤ **The dreamer must remain in charge at all times.**

Reveal only what feels comfortable. If you find you are becoming uneasy or frustrated, it might be best to temporarily stop sharing any more information about that dream.

➤ **Don't tell other people what their dreams mean.**

Dream symbols are very personal. Their significance depends upon the content of the dream as well as where and when the image appeared. What makes sense to you may not be helpful to the other dreamer.

➤ **Dreamers have a right to choose what they feel is valid.**

When sharing dreams, it is critical that no one assumes a position of authority about what the dreams might mean. When you share dreams, you are trying to offer suggestions helpful to the dreamer about what the dream or its images might mean. If the other person rejects your suggestions, that's O.K. Your job is to offer other perspectives, not conclusions.

➤ **Shared dreams must be kept confidential.**

When we share dreams, it is important that all people involved treat the information as confidential. This means no one should ever discuss the dreams with someone outside the dream-sharing group. This point is especially important if you are sharing dreams with some of your friends or family.

Dreaming Our Stress Away

By now I'm sure you've learned many things about yourself and your dreams. Perhaps you have also realized how learning to understand your dreams can put you in contact with your inner awareness—that deeper, wiser part of you.

Some of you may have figured out that if you don't listen to your dreams, they'll try to get your attention anyway. Perhaps you've had a nightmare or a strange dream that has caught your attention. Maybe you've even had a chance to finally tame one of those monsters under your bed.

That's great!

Everyone experiences stress and anxiety. You tend to dream more heavily when you feel anxious about major changes in your lives. Even positive changes such as graduating from high school, going off to college, getting married, having a baby, or starting a new job can produce anxiety. But these changes bring opportunities to learn—even if it's through our dreams.

At other times, what happens in your dream life has little in common with your waking world. Just when things seem to be at their worst in your waking life, your night life may be filled with euphoric dreams. Or when your life is at its best, you can have somber and sad dreams. Although this may seem inconsistent, dreams actually help you maintain balance in your inner world.

You know now that you can actually use your magical daydreams to visualize your future, trying out different scenarios to see which ones you like the best. You can rehearse what you need to say to your parents, teachers, and friends about the changes in your life and how you feel or think about them.

If you want, you can dream your stress away!

Lifting the Veil of Illusion

Over the years, I've thought about the "Alice and the Broken Mirrors" dream, pondering its meaning. Even from the beginning, I always knew the major message of this dream was that some things cannot and should not be explained through logic and reasoning. Magic is one of those things.

Because I became Alice in the dream, I knew that on some level, it was an initiation dream. An initiation dream assists us in breaking down old barriers or beliefs, guiding us to a new way of knowing.

In this dream, I had gone to a place where no mirrors were needed because "all is one." In that place, there was no separation of the world in front of the mirror and the world behind the mirror. In essence, the dream confirmed my belief in something that I had always known in childhood, but I had no words for—an unshakable belief about the inner-connectedness of life. It seems as if I grew up intuitively knowing that "all is one" even though no adults ever really talked with me about this in specific terms.

As a child, when I was alone with Nature, it seemed as if the trees, the animals, the rocks, and plants were speaking to me. Even though I couldn't exactly understand their language, I always knew that if I would just get very quiet, I could hear them. Perhaps you've had a similar experience. Many of us know things or learn things at a subconscious level. It's almost as if our waking minds simply cannot or will not accept certain things, so we do our learning more in silence, in sleep, and in our dreams.

If you want to bring your dreams into closer alignment with the waking world, you will need to learn a looser definition of reality. In time, you may even come to understand that there is no difference between seeing in the real world and seeing in the world of dreams. Both are different aspects of the same thing.

To dream well, you must develop a strong sense of individuality. You must be willing to be alone without being lonely. This often involves listening to your intuition rather than what logic tells you. It means developing your creativity and your creative imagination. This means giving your dreams wings to fly on their own. In time, you will learn how not to be afraid. Somewhere along the way, you'll simply learn how to hang on and enjoy the ride!

Magical Practice

Dream Protection and Relaxation

skills developed
- provides a protective field for the body
- recharges the aura by restoring its protective powers

Relaxation is crucial for any magic to happen. If you are stressed or worried, you may be keeping yourself from remembering your dreams. Stress and worry can block your intuition and your creative imagination, which is the source of your inner magic.

Progressive relaxation and rhythmic breathing are an essential part of creating a more magical life. I do this three-part exercise every night before I fall asleep. It takes me less than five minutes to complete.

This exercise will create a protective field around you so you can fall asleep without worrying about outside energies.

NOW I LAY ME
DOWN TO SLEEP...

1. **Lie flat on your back in your bed and use whatever amount of covers are needed to keep warm.**

    Close your eyes and when you begin to feel warm, your body will automatically begin to relax physically.

2. **Turn your attention to both of your feet, clenching up your toes for a second or two, and then letting them go.**

    You are focusing on relaxing the muscles in the extremities of your body.

3. **Then stretch your toes upward so they are turned towards your head and at the same time, tense the calf muscles in your lower legs.**

    Hold for a second or two, then relax.

4. **Clench your fists tightly.**

    Hold for a second or two, then relax.

Magical Practice

5. **Take in a deep breath in, starting at your tummy, and count to two: then begin to slowly exhale while counting to five.**

    Concentrating on controlling breathing helps relax and slow your intake of air to a more natural rhythm.

    Continue to breath in and out in this manner three more times.

6. **Using your imagination, see yourself surrounded by an aura of pure light.**

    If different colors appear to you, don't worry. Greet the different colors as they appear and thank them for their protection.

7. **In your mind's eye, see your head and body surrounded by a circle of light.**

    Pay attention to halo surrounding your head.

    As your body relaxes, it will unconsciously put you in a more receptive state of mind.

8. **Give thanks to the Divine for protection through the night.**

Last night I dreamed
I was a butterfly.
But today I am a man.
Am I a man
dreaming that I am a
butterfly, or a butterfly
dreaming that I am a
man?

Chuang Tzu,
Chinese philosopher and poet

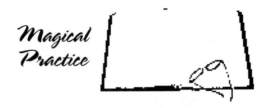

Magical Practice

Reviewing Your Dream Journal

skills developed
- promotes self-awareness
- provides fertile ground for reflective thinking

The best thing about keeping a Dream Journal is reviewing it from time to time. That way, you can get a good sense of the overall quality of your dream life. You can also see how your dreams are impacting your waking hours. By working with your dreams, you are probably now able to view your life from a different perspective. Perhaps you've even made some changes in your life due to your dreams.

If it is at all possible, you'll want to review your Dream Journal on a regular basis. If you're dreaming every night, then reviewing your Dream Journal anywhere from once a week to once a month is reasonable. Try not to go more than six weeks without reviewing your dreams. Longer than that and you'll lose touch with your dream life.

You might want to make monthly summary notes and record them in your Dream Journal. You will need

to decide how to document new insights gained when you review your Dream Journal.

Reviewing your Dream Journal on a yearly basis, on or near your birthday, helps you to see the cyclical nature of your dreams. A yearly review will also give you a larger perspective of what is going on in your dream life. Some years, it might seem like all you did was learn one lesson right after another. You can also see the months where it was easier to recall your dreams and the months that you struggled with finding solutions to your daily problems.

Many dreams may seem on the surface to predict future events or dramatic situations. Do not jump to conclusions. With practice, you will be able to discern if a dream is one of precognition (reflecting future events). As you gain experience in working with your dreams, you will become skilled at applying dream insights to your day-to-day life circumstances. And that's what dreamtime magic is all about!

Magical Practice

PULLING IT
ALL TOGETHER

1. Decide how often you want to review your Dream Journal and then be very committed to doing so.

2. As you review your dreams, look for patterns that may be appearing.

   A pattern can be characters or objects that show up frequently. Perhaps a series of dreams will have the same setting (a forest, the house you lived in when you were a child).

   These repeated dream settings can be clues as to what you are working on at a subconscious level.

3. Look for behaviors, issues, or feelings which keep popping up.

   Feelings that appear frequently in your dreams may need to be examined in your waking life as well.

   Feelings of anger, loneliness, or depression, especially if they are continually exaggerated in dreams, may be a sign of deeper issues.

4. Keep your eye out for healing or learning at a subconscious level.

Reviewing Your Dream Journal (cont.)

Some of us start learning or healing subconsciously. Until our waking minds can accept miracles, they will happen instead as we sleep.

5. **You may want to track dreams that fall into a particular category.**

    ☆ nightmares,

    ☆ psychic dreams,
    those that either seemed to be or later proved to be telepathic or precognitive in nature

    ☆ flying dreams,
    where you are flying especially, if your have some magical assistance

    ☆ out-of-body dreams, and
    those where you seem to leave your body and see it from outside yourself—such as the ceiling

    ☆ moon phases in relationship to your dreams.
    sometimes there is a difference in dreams with a full moon

Sometimes it is only after a dream has mellowed over the years that we really see how it has dramatically influenced our lives.

Suggestions for Parents

Be Grateful for All Dream Experiences

➤ **Honor the privacy of your young person's dreams.**

I realize it can be tempting to share one of your young person's dreams with a special friend, but **don't**. When young people have shared things with parents in confidence, they do not expect those things to be shared with other people—and that includes grandparents, aunts, uncles, brothers, or sisters.

It is almost never O.K. for a parent to discuss a young person's dream when he or she is not present unless the young person has given the parent permission to do so.

➤ **Perform the dream protection exercise with your young person.**

Many new clients tell me they hesitate to work with their dreams. They're afraid that if they leave their bodies during that night (astral project), they will open themselves up to negative spirits.

Small children who are plagued with nightmares may also have this concern.

➤ **Support your young person's feelings.**

Dreams often reveal what is and not what we want to see or believe. Young people sometimes experience very difficult feelings. They need caring adults like you to help them sort through things without the fear of being judged or ridiculed. Let your young person be a young person and don't expect an adult's ability to handle heavy emotional things.

Encourage and support your young people in their efforts and remind them of your love and faith in them. Often that will be enough to get them through the darkest of nights.

➤ **Maintain your own sense of wonder!**

Sometimes in life it is more important to feel than to know. By remembering how we felt and believed as a young person, we can begin to rediscover the magic and wonders of our own life and dreams.

Glossary

astral plane	level of consciousness bridging dimensions of matter and spirit; sometimes called the astral realm; the dimension of dreams, healing, and spiritual transformations
aura	the energy field surrounding all matter; around humans, the electromagnetic field
belief	pattern of thoughts shaping behavior and life; confidence in existence of something not readily seen or perceived; to know that something truly exists, often without proof
conscious mind	normal, waking state concerned with everyday activities of physical, mental, and emotional well-being
creative imagination	source of inner magic; connected with creative spirit; deeper level of mind opening doors to magical and spiritual realms of wisdom and knowledge beyond the normal way of thinking
creative visualization	the ability to create mental pictures or images in your mind's eye and hold them steady for a reasonable time; sometimes called *guided meditation* or *guided imagery*
dream incubation	a technique for requesting or programming the conscious mind to "think on" a problem while dreamer is asleep
imagination	image-making faculty of mind used in all creative activities, including magical daydreams and creative visualization

intuition	psychic perceptions; the inner knowing and feeling
lucid dreaming	dream state where dreamer is aware that dreaming is occuring; can be learned; usually occurs in REM sleep.
night terror	abrupt awakening, usually in first 2 hours, with sense of terror; not generally described by sleeper as a dream but as images or sensations; often occurs in younger children rather than adults.
sleep cycle	the approximately 90-minute period between REM and non-REM sleep.
sleep paralysis	motor inability to move legs, arms, and body during REM sleep; keeps sleeper from physically acting out the dream
sleeptalking and sleepwalking	vocalization or moving about during sleep; not usually associated with REM sleep.
subconscious mind	part of mind controling involuntary bodily functions, including reflex actions; where all memories are stored, a "personal picture dictionary"; activates specific memories, thoughts, or feelings during dream state
Universal Mind	a spiritual dimension far greater than our limited waking world
Universal Spirit	the essence commonly referred to as God or the Great Creator, sometimes called creative energy

Recommended Reading

Bethards, Betty. *The Dream Book: Symbols for Self-Understanding*. Rockport, MA: Element Books, Inc., 1995.

> A great beginner book that contains a dream dictionary listing more than 1600 common dream symbols and their meanings.

Delaney, Gayle. *In Your Dreams: Falling, Flying, and Other Dreams Themes*. San Francisco, CA: Harper-Collins, 1997.

> Delaney is well known for her "dream interview" technique for interpreting dreams. This book offers excellent suggestions on the possible meaning of different dream themes.

Kincher, Jonni. *Psychology for Kids*. Minneapolis, MN: Free Spirit Publishing, Inc. 1995.

> Contains 40 fun tests that will help you to learn more about yourself. Includes tests to determine if you have extra-sensory perception, are clairvoyant, and if you can predict the future.

Linn, Denise. *Past Lives, Present Dreams: How to Use Reincarnation for Personal Growth*. New York, NY: Ballantine, 1997.

> Linn offers practical guidance on how to address dreams that may be related to past life influences. Good information on reincarnation and specific suggestions on ways to relax.

Gillian Holloway, Ph.D. *Dreaming Insights: A 5-Step Plan for Discovering the Meaning In Your Dreams*. Portland OR: Practical Psychology Press, 1994.

> Provides a 5-step plan for discovering the meaning of your dreams. Discusses the language of dreams and shows how to improve dream recall. Excellent section of typical dream symbols and their meaning.

Tanner, Wilda. *The Mystical Magical Marvelous World of Dreams*. Tahlequah, OK: Sparrow Hawk Press, 1988.

> An extensive encyclopedia of dream symbols. Good insights on how to set up a "Dreamer's Guest Book" that can be helpful in determining who's who in your dreams.

Association for the Study of Dreams (ASD)
http://www.asdreams.org

Provides information on all regional and international events
sponsored by the ASD. Many excellent articles and helpful
publications on dreams and dreaming.

Dream Emporium
http://www.dreamemporium.com

Fun site! Good section on nightmares, night terrors, sleep walking,
and sleep talking. You can enter a contest to win a free dream
interpretation.

DreamGate
http://www.dreamgate.com

An on-line educational site that offers monthly courses on dreams,
dream sharing, dream work, and the history of dream. You can also
join a dream group via e-mail.

Dream Lynx
http://www.dreamlynx.com

Site offers a wide variety of options such as: dream technique-
a-week, dream journal, resources and theory, surveys, and research.
You can submit your dream and get feedback from other people who
provide insights into your dream by looking at it as if it were their
own dream.

Dream Network
http://www.dreamnetwork.net

Features inspiring articles by professional dream workers from the
in-print magazine by the same name. Contains a directory of
regional dream networkers (by state) who will respond to your
questions and help you join or start a dream group.

The Novato Center for Dreams
http://www.members.aol.com/dreammzzz/index.html

Good site for additional resources, books, audio, and video tapes
on dreams. The Executive Director, Jill Susan Gregory, has written
several wonderful articles on bringing dreams into the classroom.
Good site for parents, teachers, and dream-inspired artists.

Q

quartz 139
questions
  for a dream buddy 145
  for problem-solving 165

R

rapid eye movement (REM)
  18–19, 106, 241
reading list 242
  of bedtime stories 143
recurring dreams 27–28, 144
reflection 58
relaxation 134
  magical practice 230–232
religious rites 147
REM *see* rapid eye movement
repression 128, 196
research in dreams 18–19, 24
Rhiannon 195
rhythmic breathing 134, 230–232
rituals
  bedtime 133, 135, 138, 167
  Greek 147
  grounding 181
  for protection 221–223
rocks *see* stones
roles in family 50–51, 58–64,
  66–67

S

scary dreams 128
Schwarzenegger, Arnold 52
seed image 177–178
self-awareness 182–187, 212–215,
  227, 234–237
self-confidence 208–211
self-expression 120–122
self-knowledge 58
self-talk 83–84
sewing machine 148–149
sexual dreams 106, 111, 114
shaman 89, 171, 175, 223
snakes 149
soul 110
spirit
  guides, 89–90
  universal, 29
  world, 32–37
spiritual
  beings, 176
  consciousness, 183
  direction, 89–90
  evolution, 182
  teachings, 173
  stability, 133, 139
stones 138–139
  creating doorways 156–157
  for dream recall 135, 139
  for protection 194–195
stories at bedtime 141, 167
stress 131, 227–228
subconscious mind 241
symbolic dreams 107–108
symbols
  cultural 124
  defined 75
sensitivity to 94–99
sympathetic magic 141

Young Person's School of Magic and Mystery
Volume I

Magic of Believing

by

Ted Andrews

Hardbound

256 pages

$18.95 USA

ISBN 1-888767-43-X

Learn what every magician, priest, priestess, shaman, and wise one throughout history had to learn. Discover the power of imagination and belief!

In the *Magic of Believing* you will learn how:

- to make wishes come true,
- to weave a little glamour,
- to develop invisibility,
- to control the temperature,
- to awaken psychic power,
- to find lost things,
- to sail through time, and
- to create a magical life.

Now Available!

Young Person's School of Magic & Mystery
VOLUME IV

Star Magic

by

Page Bryant

Hardbound

256 pages

$18.95 USA

ISBN 1-888767-
44-8

Uncover the mystery and magic of the heavens! In *Star Magic*, you will learn how:

- to become a star shaman,
- to read the night sky,
- to create a star body,
- to meet the star people,
- to collect and use sacred star objects,
- to make a sacred star bundle,
- to awaken the magic of the sun and moon, and
- to become a starwalker.

About the Author

With a grandmother who was clairvoyant, **Pagyn Alexander** grew up in a family where being psychic was well accepted. During her formative years, family members openly discussed dreams, visions, and psychic predictions.

Pagyn's spiritual journey began with a near-death experience at eight, followed by the death of her father a week later. These life changing events propelled her into the dream world where she frequently visited with people who were no longer living.

In high school, Pagyn turned to writing poetry as a way to express insights received in dreams. Several of her dream-inspired poems have been published in literary magazines and regional poetry anthologies.

While working on her masters in creative writing, she began to explore how dreams are used for healing in other cultures, a subject she continues to research. Recently, she has focused on working with teachers and school administrators to bring dream study into the classroom environment. In this way, students will be able to benefit from using dreams as fuel for creative expression, personal growth, or career exploration.